CITY ARE BACK

DOUBLE GLORY FOR THE MINSTERMEN

CITY ARE BACK

BACK

DOUBLE GLORY
FOR THE MINSTERMEN

PAUL S. WILSON

CROFT PUBLICATIONS

First published in 2012
by Croft Publications
The Croft
8 St James Meadow
Boroughbridge
YO51 9NW

ISBN 978 0 9555126 7 4

Front cover photo: Manager Gary Mills shows his joy at winning promotion.
Courtesy Gordon Clayton.

Typeset and designed by
CROFT PUBLICATIONS
The Croft, 8 St James Meadow
Boroughbridge, YO51 9NW

Printed by
Kingsbury Press
Unit 13, Durham Lane
West Moor Park, Armthorpe
Doncaster, DN3 3FE

Bound by
Smith Settle Printing and Bookbinding Ltd
Gateway Drive, Yeadon, LS19 7XY

CONTENTS

This book is dedicated to my brother,
Neil Wilson, and my nephew, Robert Christian Wilson,
who listened from afar.

To the memory of my dear, departed mother,
who I miss so much.

INTRODUCTION

FOOTBALL!, either you are born with it, in your blood, or you are not. There is nothing in between.

Football can raise you up to such a level that you feel like the happiest person on Planet Earth, or else it can leave you virtually suicidal, it really can.

When it all comes down to it, it's really all about the "P" and "R" words, Promotion and Relegation, of course. You follow your team year after year, in the hope of going up, or else you follow them hoping to avoid the dreaded drop, in other words it's either celebration or abject misery at the end of the day, or is it really as simple as that?

Every game is so important, indeed every aspect of every game that goes towards the end result. It's every goal, every miss, every shot, every save, and so much more. It's every annoying refereeing decision, any offside decisions, free-kicks, fouls, and so much more. Every one of those things can make us want to throw our programmes on the floor in absolute disgust, or they can make us want to go straight to the Fish and Chip shop to celebrate, (in the sad case of my particular match-day moods).

You have to live it to enjoy it. In order to enjoy it you have to suffer a lot of hardships and misery along the way. (That is surely the case not just watching York City, but watching England as well). The "happy" moments are so much sweeter after you have plumbed the depths earlier. From the enjoyment of a late, late winner, to the opposite, conceding a late, late goal, football provides real life drama, in a nutshell, and it gives you the whole gamet of Human emotions in 90 minutes. There is nothing quite like it.

It is the anticipation of what could happen, or what you want to happen, that gives you the Buzz. When you have to work in the humdrum world of nine to five employment, you need something to look forward to at weekends. From the "Fish and Chips" moments to the "Programme on the floor" moments, it's what makes you tick.

I was weaned on York City since I first went to Bootham Crescent with my dad as an eight-year old. I should have been an Hartlepool fan (like my dad) but chose to swear my allegiance to the Minstermen instead.

Yes, we have had more bad seasons than good, looking at those 45 years, I suppose, but the bad times always make the good times so much sweeter.

My dear old Mum on many occasions would say to me, "I don't know why you bother going when you come home so miserable", after yet another defeat.

But you have to go don't you. Just in case. Just in case something special happened, like in 2012. That's the reward that you deserve.

We all enjoyed the ride on that roller-coaster.

ACKNOWLEDGEMENTS

I WOULD like to thank my friend Ted for his company at York City games and for suffering my mood swings. Also for supplying the photographs which appear on pages 185-190 and the back cover. My thanks also go to the *The Press,* York for all the other photographs within the book, Gordon Clayton for the front cover photograph and to Terry Nicholson at Croft Publications for his patience, time and encouragement, during the production of this book.

CHAPTER I
A BRIEF HISTORY OF YORK CITY

FOR ALL SUPPORTERS of the Minstermen, the Club's History has been well documented elsewhere.

The original YORK CITY Football Club was founded in 1908 as an Amateur side, and joined the Northern League. After 2 seasons in the Yorkshire Combination, the club turned Professional in 1912, and joined the Midlands League for the next 3 seasons, where their best position was in 10th. They played their final season in 1914-15, then folded up during World War One.

In 1922, York City reformed as a Limited Company, and regained admission to the Midland League. In the 7 years they reached their highest placing of 6th in 1925 and 1927. In 1929 the club was elected to play in the Football League.

In their first game in the League, City won away, at Wigan Borough, with goals from Stockhill and Cowie. City spent the following 22 seasons, to 1957-58 in the Third Division, North. They spent most of the time in the bottom half of the table until the 1950s, when they reached the giddy heights of 4th place in 1953 and 1955.

City performed well in Cup competitions, and built up their reputation as "Giants-Killers" in 1937-38 in the FA Cup when they knocked out First Division West Bromwich Albion (3-2) and Middlesbrough (1-0), both at Bootham Crescent. They met Huddersfield in the quarter-final at home, and drew 0-0 in front of 28,123, which remains an all-time record attendance for the club. City lost the replay 2-1 at Leeds Road.

The club's longest, and most famous cup run came in 1954-55 when they reached the semi-finals of the competition, a campaign in which Arthur Bottom scored 8 goals. The team knocked out Scarborough and Dorchester, in the early rounds, and in the 3rd round they knocked out First Division Blackpool, who included Stanley Matthews in their line-up, and had won the competition 2 years earlier. They went on to beat the famous Tottenham Hotspur in the 5th round, and won 1-0 at Notts County in the quarter-finals. In the semis they drew 1-1 with Newcastle before bowing out 2-0 in the replay at Roker Park.

In 1958, CITY became founding members of the 4th Division, as the 3rd Divisions North and South were restructured into a National League, Division 3 and 4, based on league positions in 1957-58. City unfortunately missed out on going into Division 3 on goal average, but were duly promoted in the following season to Division 3, as they finished 3rd in the inaugural season of Division 4 in 1958-59. They were relegated back down in the following season.

York's best season in the League Cup came in 1961-62 when they reached the 5th round, and lost to Rochdale, who ended up as losing finalists themselves.

In 1964-65, City were promoted again, but were once again relegated in the very next season. Their extraordinary record of being promoted every 6 years was maintained when they went up in 1970-71, helped by the performances of Phil Boyer, a future England player. They survived the drop on goal-difference for the next 2 seasons.

In 1973-74 the "Three-up, Three-down" system was initiated, and City capitalised on it. By finishing 3rd, they gained promotion to the second level of English football for the first time in their History. In their first season they played in front of the highest attendance involving City in league games; 46,802 at Manchester United on March 29th, 1975. They lost the game 2-1 but finished the season in 15th spot, their highest ever league placing. During October 1974 they were placed in 5th position in Division 2, after winning at Oldham.

The following season they finished in 21st position and were relegated. Under former Manchester United manager Wilf McGuinness the club dropped further still, into the 4th Division in 1976-77 after finishing bottom of the 3rd Division. In the 1981-82 season York endured a run of 12 home games without a win, and for the first time lost an FA Cup tie against non-league opposition as they went down 4-3 at Altrincham in the 2nd Round.

CITY won the 4th Division Championship in 1983-84, with a record 101 points. It was the first time they had won a title, and they became the first side to reach 100 points in a football league season. In January, 1985 York recorded a victory over Arsenal in the 4th round of the FA Cup after winning 1-0 at Bootham Crescent courtesy of an 89th minute penalty scored by Keith Houchen (see poem on page 25.) They proceeded to draw 1-1 with Liverpool on February 16th, 1985 but lost 7-0 in the replay at Anfield, suffering their record FA Cup defeat, (against the European Champions) The teams met again in the following season, and after another 1-1 draw at Bootham, Liverpool won 3-1 after extra-time in the replay, but not before City had had a "goal" controversially ruled out by referee Howard Taylor ten minutes from the end of normal time.

In 1993, York ended a 5-year spell in the (new) Division 3 by gaining promotion to Division 2 via the play-offs. Crewe Alexandra were beaten in the club's first ever visit to Wembley Stadium in a 5-3 penalty shoot-out win in the final. They stayed in Division 2 for 6 seasons, reaching the play-offs in their first season, but lost to Stockport County in the semi-finals, 1-0 on aggregate.

In 1995-96 York recorded a shock victory in the 2nd round of the League Cup when they beat the eventual FA Premier League Champions and FA Cup Winners, Manchester United 4-3 on aggregate, including a 3-0 win at Old Trafford in the first leg. Although United fielded 5 fringe players in the first leg, their full first team was unable to overcome the deficit at Bootham Crescent in front of 9,386. City went down 3-1 at QPR in the next round after scoring first.

City went on to beat Everton in the following season's competition, again in the 2nd round. They drew the first leg 1-1 at Goodison, and won the second leg 3-2 at Bootham Crescent.

In December, 2001 long serving Chairman Douglas Craig put the club and its ground up for sale for £4.5 million, announcing that unless a new owner was found before 1 April, 2002, City would be withdrawn from the Football League. Team B & Q racing driver and team owner John Batchelor took over as Chairman in March 2002. He promised the club he would purchase the ground and give the City supporters 24% of the shares, and that he would invite two supporters on to the Board. All these promises were found to be hollow, and all went undelivered, to the anger of the City faithful, who had no choice but to take control of the club themselves in March 2003.

In the 2003-04 season, City failed to win any of their last 20 League games, and were relegated to the Football Conference after 75 years of membership to the Football League.

Then began the wilderness years . . .

CHAPTER 2
THE NON-LEAGUE YEARS: 2004-2011

AFTER CITY'S relegation to the National Conference, manager Chris Brass, and his players received a massive vote of confidence from thousands of supporters, who invaded the pitch after losing their last home game in the Football League to Leyton Orient on the 1st of May, 2004.

Chris Brass made a stirring speech, thanking the fans for their support, and vowing that City would make every effort to get back in the Football League as quickly as they could.

A number of experienced players were brought in for the 2004-5 season with that in mind. They included Steve Davis, formerly of Burnley and Blackpool, who was made skipper, Shaun Smith from Crewe, Paul Groves from Grimsby, and Paul Robinson, who had been at Newcastle. Another well known striker, Andy Bishop was also signed from Walsall. In City's first game in the National Conference, they went down 2-0 at Aldershot, their first goal coming from a certain Jon Challinor ironically, who was to make York City his last club of nine he had played for at this level. On the following Tuesday, City won 2-0 at home to Tamworth, and recorded their first victory at the new level. The first goal for City in the Conference was scored by Paul Groves.

City struggled to find their feet, and found themselves languishing in 19th position in early November after losing 3-1 at home to Forest Green. Chris Brass was relieved of his services, and Viv Busby was made caretaker-manager for the time being.

Through the winter months City did not fare much better, they won just two more games by the end of 2004, and were lying 18th at the turn of the year.

On February 10th, Billy McEwan was announced as the new manager, his appointed task to keep City from dropping down even further down the football pyramid to the unthinkable depths of the Conference North. Ironically, his first game in charge was at Forest Green, the side who put paid to Chris Brass's days at City. After a 1-1 draw the team rallied with back to back wins against Exeter and Barnet, as they reached the giddy heights of 15th position.

City then failed to win in any of their next nine games, and lurched back down to 19th place, before winning their last game of the campaign 4-0 against a Farnborough side already consigned to relegation.

In their first season in non-league since their Midland League days of the 1920s, City had only scored 39 goals in 42 games, and they finished 17th with 43 points. Things had not quite gone as planned.

Top goal scorer was Andy Bishop with 12 goals, 11 of which came in the league. Average home attendance was 2,331.

NATIONAL CONFERENCE LEAGUE TABLE
2004-2005

											City results	
											Home	Away
1.	Barnet	42	16	2	3	56-20	10	6	5	34-24	86	w 2-1	L 0-4
2.	Hereford U	42	10	7	4	28-14	11	4	6	40-27	74	L 0-3	L 0-2
3.	Carlisle U	42	12	5	4	39-18	8	8	5	35-19	73	w 2-1	L 0-6
4.	Aldershot	42	13	3	5	38-22	8	7	6	30-30	73	L 0-2	L 0-2
5.	Stevenage B	42	13	2	6	35-21	9	4	8	30-31	72	w 3-1	D 2-2
6.	Exeter City	42	11	5	5	39-22	9	6	6	32-28	71	L 1-2	w 1-0
7.	Morecambe	42	12	5	4	38-23	7	9	5	31-27	71	w 1-0	L 1-2
8.	Woking	42	11	6	4	29-19	7	8	6	29-26	68	L 0-2	L 0-1
9.	Halifax Town	42	13	4	4	45-24	6	5	10	29-32	66	D 1-1	L 0-2
10.	Accrington S	42	11	6	4	43-26	7	5	9	29-32	65	L 0-1	D 2-2
11.	Dagenham & R	42	12	4	5	39-27	7	4	10	29-33	65	D 0-0	w 3-0
12.	Crawley T	42	13	4	4	35-18	3	5	13	15-32	57	w 3-1	L 0-1
13.	Scarborough	42	9	12	0	42-17	5	2	14	18-29	56	L 0-2	L 1-5
14.	Gravesend	42	7	7	7	34-31	6	4	11	24-33	50	D 0-0	L 0-4
15.	Tamworth	42	10	3	8	22-22	4	8	9	31-41	50	w 2-0	L 0-1
16.	Burton Alb	42	6	7	8	25-29	7	4	10	25-37	50	L 1-2	w 2-0
17.	YORK CITY	42	7	6	8	22-23	4	4	13	17-43	43		
18.	Canvey Island	42	6	10	5	34-31	3	5	13	19-34	42	D 0-0	L 0-4
19.	Northwich V	42	9	5	7	37-29	5	5	11	21-43	42	D 0-0	L 0-3
20.	Forest Green	42	2	9	10	19-40	4	6	11	22-41	33	L 1-3	D 1-1
21.	Farnborough	42	4	5	12	20-40	2	6	13	15-49	29	w 4-0	D 1-1
22.	Leigh RMI	42	2	2	17	18-52	2	4	15	13-46	18	D 1-1	w 3-0

Carlisle, who had been relegated with City in the previous season, were promoted via the play-offs, where they beat Stevenage 1-0.

NATIONAL CONFERENCE SEASON 2005-2006

Manager Billy McEwan had to bolster his squad for a shot at the play-offs in 2005. He bought striker Clayton Donaldson from Hull City, to improve the goals column; Donaldson and Bishop would be the new partnership up front.

He also brought in midfielder Manny Panther from Partick Thistle, ex Darlington winger, Mark Convery, defenders Mark Hotte from Scarborough, and Nathan Peat from Lincoln. Another defender, James Dudgeon arrived, and David McGurk returned from Darlington, after an initial spell on loan from the Quakers.

Things were looking brighter for City from the start, they went through their first four games unbeaten, until they went down 1-0 at Halifax in a match televised live.

Donaldson and Bishop were providing a useful strike force, and netted 18 goals between them in the first 15 games, in taking City to 2nd in the table by the 15th of October.

There then followed a goal drought for 5 games, in which City lost four out of five games, and they sunk to 8th by Christmas.

On Boxing Day, rivals Scarborough, who had hammered City 5-1 at their seaside home last season, were the visitors, in front of nearly 5,000 (4,921 in fact). City went a goal down, midway through the first half, until one Emmanuel Panther entered the fray. He ripped into three ferocious tackles, and within seconds of his arrival, he was booked. From that point, City won the game 3-1, inspired by Panther's spirit.

City only won one of the next seven games, however, and were firmly stuck in 8th position. In late February and early March, City then won six in a row, starting at home to Aldershot, when another Bishop, Neal, made his debut, and ending with a home win over Gravesend.

The terrific run had taken City into 4th spot, and the play-offs seemed a distinct possibility in early March. On April 4th, City won 3-0 at Altrincham, and were still handily placed in 5th, with just five games remaining.

Sadly, it was not to be, as City faltered, and failed to find a victory in any of their last five games, they finished a disappointing 8th.

Andy Bishop had scored 25 goals, and Clayton Donaldson 18, but Bishop was out of contract, and was sold to Bury in the summer.

City's average home attendance for the season was 2,871.

NATIONAL CONFERENCE LEAGUE TABLE
2005-2006

1.	Accrington S.	42	16	3	2	38-17	12	4	5	33-28	91	L 2-4	L 1-2
2.	Hereford U.	42	11	7	3	30-14	11	7	3	29-19	80	L 1-3	L 0-1
3.	Grays Ath.	42	7	9	5	46-32	14	4	3	48-23	76	L 1-2	D 1-1
4.	Halifax Town.	42	14	6	1	31-11	7	6	8	24-29	75	L 0-2	L 0-1
5.	Morecambe	42	15	4	2	44-17	7	4	10	24-24	74	D 1-1	L 0-2
6.	Stevenage B.	42	15	3	3	38-15	4	9	8	24-32	69	L 0-1	d 1-1
7.	Exeter City	42	11	3	7	41-22	7	6	8	24-26	63	w 4-2	w 3-1
8.	YORK CITY	42	10	5	6	36-26	7	7	7	27-22	63		
9.	Burton Alb.	42	8	7	6	23-31	8	5	8	27-31	60	L 0-1	D 0-0
10.	Dagenham & R.	42	8	4	9	31-32	8	6	7	32-27	58	D 1-1	w 2-0
11.	Woking.	42	8	7	6	30-20	6	7	8	28-27	56	w 2-1	L 0-2
12.	Cambridge U.	42	11	6	4	35-25	4	4	13	16-32	55	w 1-0	L 0-2
13.	Aldershot.	42	10	4	7	30-30	6	2	13	31-44	54	w 3-2	L 1-2
14.	Canvey I.	42	6	8	7	23-27	7	4	10	24-31	51	w 2-1	D 1-1
15.	Kidderminster.	42	8	5	8	21-27	5	6	10	18-28	50	D 2-2	D 0-0
16.	Gravesend.	42	8	4	9	25-25	5	6	10	20-32	49	w 1-0	D 2-2
17.	Crawley T.	42	9	4	8	27-22	3	7	11	21-33	47	D 0-0	w 1-0
18.	Southport.	42	7	3	11	24-38	3	7	11	12-30	40	D 0-0	w 4-1
19.	Forest Green.	42	7	7	7	31-27	1	7	13	18-35	38	w 5-1	w 2-1
20.	Tamworth.	42	4	10	7	17-23	4	4	13	15-40	38	w 2-1	w 3-0
21	Scarborough	42	4	7	10	24-30	5	3	13	16-36	37	w 3-1	D 2-2
22	Altrincham.	42	7	5	9	25-30	3	6	12	15-41	23	w 5-0	w 3-0

Hereford United were promoted with Accrington Stanley. Hereford beat Halifax Town 3-2 in the Play-off Final, played at Leicester.

NATIONAL CONFERENCE SEASON 2006-2007

SUBSTANTIAL changes happened at York City on June 6th, 2006. As Supporters Trust members since 2003, the McGill family, under the business name of 'JM Packaging', became the new owners of York City FC. Steve Beck, the Chairman of the trust, recommended to the 1,250 members that this was the best course of action for the club to take. Rob McGill, and his son Jason, and daughter Sophie had been avid supporters of the club since the 1950s. York City was in safe hands.

Billy McEwan was ever keen to improve his squad, for what many thought would be a serious bid for promotion in this, City's third season in the Conference. In came keeper Tom Evans from Scunthorpe, Darren Craddock from Hartlepool, and experienced midfielder Steve Bowey, from Queen of the South. One-time Leeds striker, Craig Farrell also joined, and young Welsh defender Danny Parslow arrived from Cardiff City to partner permanent signing David McGurk at the back. A fast and skillful winger, Martyn Woolford had also arrived from Frickley Athletic.

City made an excellent start, drawing 0-0 with Exeter at home, then winning the next three games to go top of the embryo table. There then followed a three game period without a win.

City kept up the momentum, especially on their travels where they won five of their first seven, and ended up with 13 away wins, equalling their record. City were never out of the top five from November onwards, and were sitting in 3rd spot at Christmas 2006.

On New Years Day, 2007 they had a useful 3-1 win at Morecambe to make it their 8th away success, and they stayed in that position until the end of February, after hitting 5 against Crawley in the first week of January, which included a rare goal by Manny Panther.

A hat-trick by Clayton Donaldson at Cambridge helped City to a 5-0 win there, before a mini-slump when just two points were gained in the next four games.

City duly won four of their last five games to gain the play-off spot they deserved, and their home victory, 1-0 over 2nd place Oxford in their last game of the season put them in good spirits for the confrontations with Morecambe in May.

A crowd of 6,660 watched a 0-0 draw at home to Morecambe in the first leg, which City dominated and had the better chances but failed to put them away.

In the second leg, at Christie Park, City took the lead with a penalty from Steve Bowey but Morecambe came back before the break, and clinched the winner early in the second half to break City hearts.

Morecambe won the play-off Final, beating Exeter City at the New Wembley Stadium.

Clayton Donaldson was top scorer with 26 goals (24 in the league), and average home attendance was 2,859.

NATIONAL CONFERENCE LEAGUE TABLE
2006-2007

		P	W	D	L	F-A	W	D	L	F-A	Pts		
1.	Dagenham & R	46	16	4	3	50-20	12	7	4	43-28	95	L 2-3	L 1-2
2.	Oxford U	46	11	9	3	33-16	11	6	6	33-17	81	w 1-0	L 1-2
3.	Morecambe	46	11	7	5	29-20	12	5	6	35-26	81	L 2-3	w 3-1
4.	YORK CITY	46	10	6	7	29-22	13	5	5	36-23	80		
5.	Exeter City	46	14	7	2	39-19	8	5	10	28-29	78	D 0-0	D 1-1
6.	Burton Alb	46	13	3	7	28-21	9	6	8	24-26	75	w 3-2	w 2-1
7.	Gravesend & N	46	12	6	5	33-25	9	5	9	30-31	74	L 0-2	w 1-0
8.	Stevenage B	46	12	4	7	46-30	8	6	9	30-36	70	L 0-1	w 2-1
9.	Aldershot T	46	11	7	5	40-31	7	4	12	24-31	65	w 1-0	w 2-0

10.	Kidderminster............	46	7	5	11	19-26	10	7	6	24-24	63	w 1-0 L 1-2
11.	Weymouth..................	46	12	6	5	35-26	6	3	14	21-47	63	w 1-0 w 2-1
12.	Rushden & D	46	10	5	8	34-24	7	6	10	24-30	62	w 3-1 w 1-0
13.	Northwich V...............	46	9	2	12	26-33	9	2	12	25-36	58	w 2-1 w 2-1
14.	Forest Green	46	10	5	8	34-33	3	13	7	25-31	57	D 0-0 w 1-0
15.	Woking	46	8	8	7	34-26	7	4	12	22-35	57	L 0-1 w 2-1
16.	Halifax Town	46	12	8	3	40-22	3	2	18	15-40	55	w 2-0 D 1-1
17.	Cambridge U...............	46	8	4	11	34-33	7	6	10	23-33	55	L 1-2 w 5-0
18.	*Crawley T	46	10	6	7	27-20	7	6	10	25-32	53	w 5-0 L 0-3
19.	Grays Ath...................	46	8	9	6	29-21	5	4	14	27-34	52	D 2-2 D 0-0
20.	Stafford R	46	7	4	12	25-33	7	6	10	24-38	52	D 0-0 D 0-0
21.	Altrincham..................	46	9	4	10	28-32	4	8	11	25-35	51	w 1-0 w 4-0
22.	Tamworth....................	46	8	6	9	24-27	5	3	15	19-34	48	L 0-2 D 2-2
23.	Southport....................	46	7	4	12	29-30	4	10	9	28-37	47	D 2-2 w 1-0
24.	St Albans	46	5	5	13	28-49	5	5	13	29-40	40	D 0-0 L 2-4

* Crawley Town were deducted 10 points

NATIONAL CONFERENCE SEASON 2007-2008

City lost star striker Clayton Donaldson, who joined Hibernian, after signing a "Pre-Contract" agreement earlier, and Neal Bishop joined Barnet. McEwan signed Onome Sodje, a striker from Gravesend and Northfleet, defender Mark Robinson from Torquay, and midfielder Stuart Elliott from Northwich Victoria. Later, after the season started, City signed centre-back Darren Kelly from Derry City, who was a former Northern Ireland under-21 International. City were hopeful of a promotion push once again, in their 4th Conference season.

But it wasn't to be. The goals of Clayton Donaldson were sorely missed, although winger Martyn Woolford was scoring a few, and a young chap called Richard Brodie from the North-east, was starting to make a name for himself.

After an abysmal start, City had only managed to win one of their first ten games, and they were leaking goals by the bucketful, having conceded 21 in that time. They were in big trouble, lying 20th in the table, and hovering on the brink of the relegation zone. Billy McEwan was under pressure.

In September and October, City made a mini-rally to win four out of the next six games against Grays, Halifax, Stafford and Woking to give themselves a little breathing space. They clobbered Rushall Olympic 6-0 in the FA Cup 4th qualifying round, and then put four past Farsley on November the 4th. After losing at home to Salisbury, 3-1 on November 17th, following a home defeat in the FA Cup to Havant and Waterlooville, City were in trouble in 19th position, and the Board was not happy.

Billy McEwan was sacked after 2½ years, and Colin Walker, his assistant, took up the reins. He started with a win at Weymouth, though to be fair, he wasn't officially in charge by then.

Under Walker, City made substantial improvements, and moved up to a respectable 10th position by the end of 2007 with four wins out of five, and Walker was given the manager's job on a permanent basis. City went from strength to strength, and finished up going eleven league games undefeated between late November and early February. City were still safe in 10th spot by that time.

Success came in the FA Trophy. For the first time City reached the semi-finals, beating Altrincham, Grays, Farsley, and Rushden along the way. Having lost the first leg of the semis 2-0 at Torquay, City won the return leg 1-0, but unluckily missed out on the Final.

City's season slumped a little after that, and they were given a 6-1 thumping by Crawley in April. Their mid-table position of 14th was a recovery from their early worries, but they needed to get back in the play-offs, or better, next time.

Onome Sodje and Martyn Woolford finished up as joint-top scorers on 17, and the average home attendance was down to 2,258.

NATIONAL CONFERENCE LEAGUE TABLE
2007-2008

		P	W	D	L		W	D	L		Pts		
1.	Aldershot T	46	18	2	3	44-21	13	6	4	38-27	101	w 2-0	L 0-2
2.	Cambridge U	46	14	6	3	36-17	11	5	7	32-24	86	L 1-2	L 0-2
3.	Torquay U	46	15	3	5	39-21	11	5	7	44-36	86	L 0-1	D 0-0
4.	Exeter City	46	13	9	1	44-26	9	8	6	39-32	83	w 3-2	D 1-1
5.	Burton Alb	46	15	3	5	48-31	8	9	6	31-25	81	d 0-0	L 3-4
6.	Stevenage B	46	13	5	5	47-25	11	2	10	35-30	79	L 0-2	L 2-3
7.	Histon	46	10	7	6	42-36	10	5	8	34-31	72	L 1-4	L 1-3
8.	Forest Green	46	11	6	6	45-34	8	8	7	31-25	71	L 0-2	w 2-1
9.	Oxford U	46	10	8	5	32-21	10	3	10	24-27	71	L 0-1	D 1-1
10.	Grays Ath	46	11	6	6	35-23	8	7	8	23-24	70	w 2-0	w 2-0
11.	Ebbsfleet U	46	14	3	6	40-29	5	9	9	25-32	69	L 0-1	w 2-1
12.	Salisbury C	46	12	7	4	35-22	6	7	10	35-38	68	L 1-3	L 0-3
13.	Kidderminster	46	12	5	6	38-23	7	5	11	36-34	67	D 2-2	L 1-3
14.	YORK CITY	46	8	5	10	33-34	9	6	8	38-40	62		
15.*	Crawley T	46	12	5	6	47-31	7	4	12	26-36	60	D 1-1	L 1-6
16.	Rushden & D	46	7	10	6	26-22	8	4	11	29-33	59	L 2-3	D 1-1
17.	Woking	46	7	9	7	28-27	5	8	10	25-34	53	L 2-3	w 3-0
18.	Weymouth	46	7	5	11	24-34	4	8	11	29-39	46	w 2-0	w 2-1
19.	Northwich V	46	6	7	10	30-36	5	4	14	22-42	44	D 1-1	w 2-1
20.*	Halifax Town	46	8	10	5	30-29	4	6	13	31-41	42	w 3-2	D 2-2
21.	Altrincham	46	6	6	11	32-44	3	8	12	24-38	41	D 2-2	D 2-2
22.	Farsley	46	6	5	12	27-38	4	4	15	21-48	39	w 4-1	w 4-1
23.	Stafford R	46	2	4	17	16-48	3	6	14	26-51	25	w 2-0	w 4-0
24.	Droylsden	46	4	5	14	27-45	1	4	18	19-58	24	w 2-1	w 4-3

* Crawley Town and Halifax were deducted 10 points

Exeter City beat Cambridge 1-0 in the play-off Final

NATIONAL CONFERENCE SEASON 2008-2009

Colin Walker had the intention of assembling a squad of 18 "quality" players for the 2008-09 campaign, in view of the limited budget he had at his disposal.

In came experienced defender or midfield player Mark Greaves from Burton Albion, and City re-signed former Northern Ireland International keeper Michael Ingham from Hereford, who had earlier been loaned to City in 2003. A lot was expected of 21-year old striker, Richard Brodie who had netted 14 goals in his first full season in the first team in 2007-08.

Also recruited by Colin Walker were four players released from the defunct Gretna, who had lost their existence in the Scottish League after reaching the Scottish Premiership in 2007, but going bankrupt in their first season at the top. The new recruits were Steven Hogg, a midfielder, as was Niall Henderson, and Ben Wilkinson, the son of Howard, the well-known manager. Also, young Polish keeper Artur Krysiak was loaned to City, but he only lasted a game and a half after being taken off injured during his home debut for City against Wrexham.

City won their first two games, then drew the next five, in a mediocre start to the campaign. They then managed only two wins in a twelve-game spell from mid-September to late November, and they slumped to 15th in the table. Colin Walker was relieved of his duties in late November, having taken City as far as he could. They later appointed Martin Foyle as the new man, who had been an experienced striker at Port Vale.

Sadly, things went from bad to worse, initially, in the League at any rate, as City struggled on. By the turn of the year, they had slumped to 16th, as they only won once in seven outings after Foyle arrived.

City were having a good run in the Trophy again, with wins against Northwich, and Oxford away. Another new striker, Daniel

McBreen, in tandem with the emerging Brodie, had scored seven goals between them in the Trophy, up to the Kidderminster tie, which City won 13-12 on penalties, after a replay at home, and including the quarter-final win at home to Havant and Waterlooville, the team who had dumped us out of the FA Cup in the previous season.

The semi-final draw paired us with Conference North side, AFC Telford. The Minstermen won 2-0 in the first leg in Shropshire, then managed a fairly comfortable 2-1 win at home in the return, with Brodie scoring his 4th in the tournament, and sending City to Wembley.

It was all a distraction from bad things happening in the League, though. By the end of March, City were really in dire straits, and had sunk to 20th, just outside the relegation zone after winning only eight games in the League all season. The first four games of April brought only two more points, and City found themselves in 22nd position on April 13th after their usual 0-0 draw at Barrow. (Every one of City's four games in the Conference played at Holker Street finished 0-0).

There was no doubt that City were in real danger of going down to the Conference North, and all the doom and gloom that it would bring to the club. The next two home games were crucial. Thankfully City won them both, beating Eastbourne 1-0 in a scrappy game, then Forest Green just 3 days later, with goals by Adam Boyes and Richard Brodie, and City were almost safe. A nervy win at troubled club Weymouth, finally pulled City mercifully clear, and they signed off with a 1-1 draw at bottom club, Lewes. But it was close, so close to the end for City.

At least the team, and their supporters could look forward to the FA Trophy Final against Stevenage, at Wembley. It was no surprise when Stevenage won 2-0 but it was a great day out anyway, after such a nervy end to their fifth season in the National Conference.

Richard Brodie top-scored with 19, including 4 in the Trophy, and the average home attendance was 2,295.

NATIONAL CONFERENCE LEAGUE TABLE
2008-2009

		P	W	D	L		W	D	L		Pts		
1.	Burton Alb	46	15	5	3	48-23	12	2	9	33-29	88	L 1-3	L 1-2
2.	Cambridge U	46	14	6	3	34-15	10	8	5	31-24	86	D 0-0	L 0-1
3.	Histon	46	14	8	1	41-18	9	6	8	37-30	83	D 1-1	D 1-1
4.	Torquay Utd	46	11	7	5	38-23	12	7	4	34-24	83	L 1-2	D 1-1
5.	Stevenage B	46	12	8	3	41-23	11	4	8	32-31	81	L 0-2	D 3-3
6.	Kidderminster	46	16	2	5	40-18	7	8	8	29-30	79	D 0-0	L 0-2
7.	Oxford U *	46	16	3	4	42-20	8	7	8	30-31	77	D 0-0	L 0-1
8.	Kettering T	46	12	5	6	26-19	9	8	6	24-18	76	D 0-0	L 2-4
9.	Crawley T *	46	13	5	5	48-26	6	9	8	29-29	70	D 2-2	W 1-0
10.	Wrexham	46	11	7	5	39-22	7	5	11	25-26	66	W 1-0	L 1-3
11.	Rushden & D	46	11	5	7	30-24	5	10	8	31-26	63	W 2-0	L 0-2
12.	Mansfield T	46	14	5	4	35-19	5	4	14	22-36	62	D 1-1	L 0-1
13.	Eastbourne B	46	11	3	9	29-27	7	3	13	29-43	60	W 1-0	L 1-2
14.	Ebbsfleet U	46	10	9	4	28-19	6	1	16	24-41	58	W 3-1	D 0-0
15.	Altrincham	46	9	7	7	30-29	6	4	13	19-37	56	L 1-2	D 1-1
16.	Salisbury City	46	8	6	9	29-33	6	7	10	25-31	55	D 1-1	D 1-1
17.	YORK CITY	46	8	9	6	26-20	3	10	10	21-31	52		
18.	Forest Green	46	7	6	10	39-40	5	10	8	31-36	52	W 2-1	D 1-1
19.	Grays Ath	46	12	5	6	31-24	2	5	16	13-40	52	L 0-1	L 0-1
20.	Barrow	46	7	10	6	27-26	5	5	13	24-39	51	D 1-1	D 0-0
21.	Woking	46	6	8	9	21-29	4	6	13	16-31	44	W 2-0	W 2-0
22.	Northwich V	46	7	5	11	29-26	4	5	14	27-49	43	L 1-2	D 2-2
23.	Weymouth	46	5	6	12	27-53	6	4	13	18-33	43	W 2-0	W 2-1
24.	Lewes	46	5	2	16	15-41	1	4	18	13-48	24	W 3-0	D 1-1

*Crawley were deducted 1 point, and Oxford were deducted 5 points.

Torquay United won the play-offs, beating Cambridge in the Final, 2-0.

NATIONAL CONFERENCE SEASON 2009-2010

Martin Foyle was still at the helm, after his first season in charge had been traumatic in the League. City had finished 17th in the end, and escaped relegation by 8 points in the final reckoning, but it was close, until the last two games. Everyone hoped for better things in Foyle's first full season, and City's sixth in the Conference.

There were numerous signings made. Full-back James Meredith from Telford, striker Michael Gash from Ebbsfleet, after long discussions on the transfer price. Midfielders Alex Lawless, Chris Carruthers, and Neil Barrett, who had been on Chelsea's books, Michael Rankine, another striker, Andy Ferrell, and Craig Nelthorpe, to name a few. Much brighter things were expected this time.

Newcomers to the Conference were Luton Town, who, having being docked a massive 30 points, were inevitably consigned to football at this level, no matter how unfair it seemed to their supporters.

After gaining five points in the first five, games, City were once again struggling early on. From late August to early October they went on a ten-game unbeaten run which put them in the play-off spots in 4th place, and things were looking good, until Bogey side Salisbury beat City 1-0 at their place. New defender Djoumin Sangare scored a dramatic late equaliser against Stevenage at home during that run.

City's first encounter at Kenilworth Road at this level ended in a 1-1 draw after Neil Barrett had given City a first half lead. Luton were always up there with the play-off chasing sides, City included, as expected.

City then won six in a row between November, and early December, but the 3-2 win over Chester was later expunged as the Cheshire club folded.

A draw at Hinckley in the FA Trophy stopped the sequence, but City made it an incredible nine league wins on the trot, by winning 1-0 at Cambridge on January 23, to put them firmly into 3rd place in the table. During this run, the Minstermen had also enjoyed FA Cup wins over Bedworth United, League 2 side Crewe, and Cambridge. They finally bowed out proudly at the Britannia Stadium, Stoke having had to journey through snow-storms on the way.

Things were looking good, and hopes of City reaching their second play-offs at this level were high. Histon stopped City's winning sequence in the League with a 1-1 draw in Cambridgeshire, and Ebbsfleet inflicted City's first defeat on them in 13 games. Luton came to Bootham Crescent on February 16th and drew 0-0.

City then had a mini-blip, and failed to win in six games, they dropped out of the play-offs into 6th spot, and still had eleven games remaining. Five wins out of the next six brought them back into 4th place with four games left, including a magnificent thumping of Wimbledon, at home by 5-0. After winning just one of the last four games, City finished 5th, and would face Luton in the play-offs.

A crowd of 6,204 saw City beat their latest rivals 1-0 at home by virtue of a stunning last minute goal by Richard Brodie. In the second leg, Chris Carruthers netted early in the second half, and City won 2-0 on aggregate. Luton fans, unhappy at having to face another season in the Conference invaded the pitch, as their season ended in despair.

Sadly, City could not go on to win the play-off Final. They went down 3-1 to Oxford after surrendering two early goals, and never really recovering, despite a second half rally.

Top scorer was Richard Brodie who netted a magnificent total of 37, all told, though 3 against Chester would not count. Average home Attendance was up to 2,639.

NATIONAL CONFERENCE LEAGUE TABLE
2009-2010

1.	Stevenage	44	16	5	1	44-11	14	4	4	35-13	99	D 1-1 L 0-1
2.	Luton Town	44	14	3	5	54-22	12	7	3	30-18	88	D 0-0 D 1-1
3.	Oxford Utd	44	16	4	2	37-10	9	7	6	27-21	88	D 1-1 L 1-2
4.	Rushden & D	44	12	6	4	40-21	10	7	5	37-18	79	D 0-0 W 1-0
5.	YORK CITY	44	13	7	2	40-15	9	5	8	22-20	78	
6.	Kettering	44	6	8	8	27-23	12	4	6	24-18	66	W 2-0 W 1-0
7.	Crawley T	44	14	3	5	33-24	5	6	11	17-33	66	W 2-0 L 1-3
8.	Wimbledon	44	8	5	9	30-19	10	5	7	31-28	64	W 5-0 W 1-0
9.	Mansfield T	44	9	8	5	34-22	8	3	11	35-38	62	W 3-0 W 1-0
10.	Cambridge U	44	11	4	7	44-24	4	10	8	21-29	59	D 2-2 W 1-0
11.	Wrexham	44	9	7	6	26-17	6	6	10	19-22	58	W 2-1 L 0-1
12.	Salisbury C	44	11	5	6	33-21	10	0	12	25-42	58	L 1-2 L 0-1
13.	Kidderminster	44	11	3	8	31-21	4	9	9	26-31	57	W 3-2 W 1-0
14.	Altrincham	44	7	7	8	29-25	6	8	8	26-26	54	W 2-1 D 0-0
15.	Barrow	44	7	9	6	27-29	6	4	12	23-38	52	W 3-0 D 0-0
16.	Tamworth	44	7	6	9	26-30	4	10	8	16-22	49	D 1-1 W 3-2
17.	Hayes & Y	44	7	7	8	38-38	5	5	12	21-47	48	W 4-1 D 1-1
18.	Histon	44	6	9	7	24-28	5	4	13	20-39	46	W 3-1 D 1-1
19.	Eastbourne	44	8	7	7	26-29	3	6	13	16-43	46	L 0-1 L 1-3
20.	Gateshead	44	10	3	9	24-23	3	4	15	22-46	45	W 1-0 W 2-1
21.	Forest Green	44	9	5	8	27-29	3	4	15	23-47	45	W 2-0 L 1-2
22.	Ebbsfleet U	44	7	4	11	25-36	5	4	13	25-46	44	W 1-0 L 0-1
23.	Grays Ath	44	4	5	13	16-41	1	8	13	19-50	26	D 1-1 W 4-0

NATIONAL CONFERENCE SEASON 2010-2011

This time, Martin Foyle's newcomers were more modest acquisitions. In came full-back Duaine Courtney from Kidderminster, and centre back Greg Young from Altrincham, midfielder Jonathan Smith, and winger Peter Till, to name a few. Unfortunately, new striker George

Purcell was injured in pre-season, and only managed one appearance as substitute for the club.

Basically, goals were hard to come by. City managed only one win in their first six games, against lowly Altrincham, and were in 16th place in the early table. They stuttered along in September, winning three, and creeping up to 10th, but went on to lose three in a row, culminating in a 4-0 thrashing at newcomers Newport County.

It marked the end of Martin Foyle's reign, as he was released by the club following that defeat.

New manager Gary Mills was appointed on October the 13th, and he immediately made his mark as City went on another impressive run in the FA Cup. After winning 2-0 at Kidderminster, they despatched League Two side Rotherham 3-0 at home in a replay, then went to Darlington and secured a 2-0 win in the depths of a winter freeze. For the second season in a row they bowed out at a Premiership club, this time at Bolton's Reebok stadium to two late goals. Once again they received plaudits from a top level manager for their efforts in the competition.

The League form was again less than impressive, though. A handy 3-0 win at Gateshead, just before the Bolton game kept them in mid table. Gary Mills brought in Scott Kerr, a midfielder from Lincoln, and Jamie Reed, a striker from Bangor City, in the New Year. Both had reasonable success in the last three months of the season, Kerr was a steadying influence in midfield, and Reed came off the bench on numerous occasions to bolster a late run for the play-offs in February and March, as City climbed to 7th in the table. City reached the fringe of the play-offs with a 1-0 win over rivals Luton on April 19th, and they had recovered from their 5-0 thrashing at Kenilworth Road. In spite of only losing three of their last 17 games, City's season ended with a defeat at Darlington, and draws against Cambridge and Crawley, finishing in a disappointing 8th position after promising so much. The signs were good for next season, though.

Top scorer was Michael Rankine with 14. Average home attendance: 2,482.

NATIONAL CONFERENCE LEAGUE TABLE
2010-2011

		P	W	D	L	F-A	W	D	L	F-A	Pts		
1.	Crawley Town	46	18	3	2	57-19	13	9	1	36-11	105	D 1-1	D 1-1
2.	Wimbledon	46	17	3	3	46-15	10	6	7	37-32	90	W 4-1	L 0-1
3.	Luton Town	46	14	7	2	57-17	9	8	6	28-20	84	W 1-0	L 0-5
4.	Wrexham	46	13	7	3	36-24	9	8	6	30-25	81	D 1-1	D 1-1
5.	Fleetwood T	46	12	8	3	35-19	10	4	9	33-23	78	W 1-0	L 1-2
6.	Kidderminster	46	13	6	4	40-27	7	11	5	34-33	72	L 1-2	D 0-0
7.	Darlington	46	13	6	4	37-14	5	11	7	24-28	71	D 0-0	L 1-2
8.	YORK CITY	46	14	6	3	31-13	5	8	10	24-37	71		
9.	Newport Co	46	11	7	5	44-29	7	8	8	34-31	69	W 2-1	L 0-4
10.	Bath City	46	10	10	3	38-27	6	5	12	26-41	63	D 1-1	D 2-2
11.	Grimsby Town	46	7	12	4	37-28	8	5	10	35-34	62	W 1-0	D 0-0
12.	Rushden & D	46	10	6	7	37-27	6	8	9	28-35	62	W 2-0	W 4-0
13.	Mansfield T	46	9	6	8	40-37	8	4	11	33-38	61	W 2-1	L 0-5
14.	Kettering	46	8	8	7	33-32	7	5	11	31-43	58	L 0-1	D 1-1
15.	Gateshead	46	8	9	6	28-28	6	6	11	35-37	57	W 2-1	W 3-0
16.	Hayes/Yeading	46	10	2	11	34-38	5	4	14	23-43	51	W 2-0	W 2-1
17.	Cambridge	46	7	7	9	32-28	4	10	9	21-33	50	D 0-0	L 1-2
18.	Barrow	46	9	6	8	31-22	3	8	12	21-45	50	D 0-0	D 0-0
19.	Tamworth	46	6	8	9	34-41	6	5	12	28-42	49	L 1-2	W 3-1
20.	Forest Green	46	7	10	6	28-25	3	6	14	25-47	46	W 2-1	L 1-2
21.	Southport	46	9	6	8	39-33	2	7	14	17-44	46	W 2-0	L 0-4
22.	Altrincham	46	6	8	9	29-38	5	3	15	18-49	44	W 3-0	D 0-0
23.	Eastbourne B	46	6	5	12	36-46	4	4	15	26-58	39	W 1-0	L 1-2
24.	Histon	46	4	3	16	18-45	4	6	13	23-45	28	W 1-0	W 2-1

AFC Wimbledon won the play-off Final against Luton on penalties at Old Trafford, Manchester.

SUMMARY OF CITY'S GAMES AGAINST NATIONAL CONFERENCE SIDES 2004 - 2012
(LEAGUE GAMES ONLY)

Team	P	W	D	L	F-A	W	D	L	F-A	W	D	L	F-A	Pts
ACCRINGTON STANLEY	4	0	0	2	2-5	0	1	1	3-4	0	1	3	5-9	1
AFC TELFORD	2	0	0	1	0-1	0	1	0	0-0	0	1	1	0-1	1
AFC WIMBLEDON	4	2	0	0	9-1	1	0	1	1-1	3	0	1	10-2	9
ALDERSHOT	8	3	0	1	6-4	1	0	3	3-6	4	0	4	9-10	12
ALFRETON T	2	0	0	1	0-1	1	0	0	2-0	1	0	1	2-1	3
ALTRINCHAM	12	4	1	1	14-5	2	4	0	10-3	6	5	1	24-8	23
BARROW	8	2	2	0	7-2	0	4	0	0-0	2	6	0	7-2	12
BARNET	2	1	0	0	2-1	0	0	1	0-4	1	0	1	2-5	3
BATH CITY	4	1	1	0	2-1	1	1	0	3-2	2	2	0	5-3	8
BRAINTREE T	2	1	0	0	6-2	1	0	0	1-0	2	0	0	7-2	6
BURTON ALBION	10	1	1	3	5-8	2	1	2	8-7	3	2	5	13-15	11
CAMBRIDGE UTD	14	1	4	2	7-8	3	0	4	8-7	4	4	6	15-15	16
CANVEY ISLAND	4	1	1	0	2-1	0	1	1	1-5	1	2	1	3-6	5
CARLISLE UTD	2	1	0	0	2-1	0	0	1	0-6	1	0	1	2-7	3
CRAWLEY TOWN	14	3	4	0	14-5	2	1	4	5-14	5	5	4	19-19	20
DAGENHAM & R	6	0	2	1	3-4	2	0	1	6-2	2	2	2	9-6	8
DARLINGTON	4	0	2	0	2-2	0	1	1	3-4	0	3	1	5-6	3
DROYLSDEN	2	1	0	0	2-1	1	0	0	4-3	2	0	0	6-4	6
EASTBOURNE BOR	6	2	0	1	2-1	0	0	3	3-7	2	0	4	5-8	6
EXETER CITY	8	2	1	1	8-6	2	2	0	6-3	4	3	1	14-9	15
FARNBOROUGH T	2	1	0	0	4-0	0	1	0	1-1	1	1	0	5-1	4
FARSLEY CELTIC	2	1	0	0	4-1	1	0	0	4-1	2	0	0	8-2	6
FLEETWOOD T	4	1	0	1	1-1	0	1	1	1-2	1	1	2	2-3	4
FOREST GREEN	16	5	1	2	13-8	3	3	2	10-9	8	4	4	23-17	28
GATESHEAD	6	2	0	1	4-3	2	0	1	7-4	4	0	2	11-7	12
GRAVESEND/EBBSFLEET	14	4	1	2	8-6	3	2	2	7-9	7	3	4	15-15	24
GRAYS ATHLETIC	10	1	2	2	6-6	2	2	1	7-2	3	4	3	13-8	13
GRIMSBY TOWN	4	2	0	0	3-1	1	1	0	3-2	3	1	0	6-3	10
HALIFAX TOWN	8	2	1	1	6-5	0	2	2	3-6	2	3	3	9-11	9

HAYES & YEADING	6	3	0	0	8-1	2	1	0	7-4	5	1	0	15-5	16
HEREFORD UNITED	4	0	0	2	1-6	0	0	2	0-3	0	0	4	1-9	0
HISTON	8	2	1	1	6-6	1	2	1	5-6	3	3	2	11-12	12
KETTERING	8	2	1	1	9-1	2	1	1	9-6	4	2	2	18-7	14
KIDDERMINSTER	14	2	3	2	11-11	1	3	3	3-8	3	6	5	14-19	15
LEIGH RMI	2	0	1	0	1-1	1	0	0	3-0	1	1	0	4-1	4
LEWES	2	1	0	0	3-0	0	1	0	1-1	1	1	0	4-1	4
LINCOLN CITY	2	1	0	0	2-0	1	0	0	2-0	2	0	0	4-0	6
LUTON TOWN	6	2	1	0	4-0	1	1	1	3-7	3	2	1	7-7	11
MANSFIELD TOWN	8	2	2	0	8-4	1	1	2	2-7	3	3	2	10-11	12
MORECAMBE	6	1	1	1	4-4	1	0	2	4-5	2	1	3	8-9	7
NEWPORT COUNTY	4	1	1	0	3-2	0	0	2	1-6	1	1	2	4-8	4
NORTHWICH VICT	8	1	2	1	4-4	2	1	1	6-7	3	3	2	10-11	12
OXFORD UNITED	8	1	2	1	2-2	0	1	3	2-6	1	3	4	4-8	6
RUSHDEN & D	10	3	1	1	9-4	3	1	1	7-3	6	2	2	16-7	20
ST ALBANS	2	0	1	0	0-0	0	0	1	2-4	0	1	1	2-4	1
SALISBURY CITY	6	0	1	2	3-6	0	1	2	1-5	0	2	4	4-11	2
SCARBOROUGH	4	1	0	1	3-3	0	1	1	3-7	1	1	2	6-10	4
SOUTHPORT	8	1	2	1	5-4	2	1	1	6-6	3	3	2	11-10	12
STAFFORD R	4	1	1	0	2-0	1	1	0	4-0	2	2	0	6-0	8
STEVENAGE B.	12	1	1	4	4-8	1	3	2	10-11	2	4	6	14-19	10
STOCKPORT CO	2	1	0	0	2-1	1	0	0	2-1	2	0	0	4-2	6
TAMWORTH	12	2	2	2	6-6	3	1	2	12-8	5	3	4	18-14	18
TORQUAY U	4	0	0	2	1-3	0	2	0	1-1	0	2	2	2-4	2
WEYMOUTH	6	3	0	0	5-0	3	0	0	6-3	6	0	0	11-3	18
WOKING	10	2	0	3	6-7	3	0	2	7-4	5	0	5	13-11	15
WREXHAM	8	2	2	0	4-2	1	1	2	5-5	3	3	2	9-7	12

NOW, WE'RE IN THE FINAL MINUTE,
WE WAIT WITH BATED BREATH.
WILL IT BE A REPLAY
OR WILL WE SNATCH ONE AT THE DEATH?
KEITH(Y) HOUCHEN'S IN THE MIDDLE
WAITING FOR THE BALL
STEVIE WILLIAMS CHASES HARD
HE'S GOT NO CHANCE AT ALL
HE COST THEM HALF A MILLION
THEY CALLED HIM STEVIE WONDER
NOW HE'S GOT A BRAND NEW NAME
IT'S LITTLE STEVIE BLUNDER
KEITH GOES DOWN INSIDE THE BOX
PENALTY ! WE SHOUT
THE FANS ALL KNOW IT, THE PLAYERS KNOW IT
AND THERE CAN BE NO DOUBT
SECONDS LATER ITS ALL OVER
LUKIC DIVES TO LEFT
THE BALL IS SITTING IN THE NET.
ARSENAL ARE BEREFT
LONDON'S PRIDE IS LEFT IN TATTERS
CITY FANS GO WILD
THERE'S NOT A DRY EYE IN THE HOUSE
WOMAN, MAN OR CHILD.

YORK CITY 1, ARSENAL 0   26 JANUARY 1985.

A POEM WRITTEN BY PAUL WILSON.

CHAPTER 3
AUGUST 2011: KEEPING THE FAITH

AFTER an arduous pre-season of no less than 9 friendlies, the most recent being a feisty 1-1 draw at Halifax and a narrow defeat at the hands of Premiership club Bolton by 1-0, the new season in the Blue Square Conference was all set to start again on August 13th, at re-vitalised Ebbsfleet, fresh from their promotion from the Blue Square South.

Most of the City faithful were delighted with the players Gary Mills had signed during the close season, and our hopes were higher than they had ever been for a real chance of promotion back to the Football League in this, our 8th campaign of Non-League football obscurity.

Jason Walker had been captured from our arch-rivals Luton Town. He had never really settled at Kenilworth Road, and his popularity hadn't been enhanced after he missed a crucial penalty in the play-off Final shoot-out last season. We hoped he would be a snip at £60,000. Time would tell.

Patrick McLaughlin, a promising 20-year old Northern Ireland under 21 International midfielder from Newcastle, and speedy 21 year old winger Matty Blair from Kidderminster, had also arrived at the Crescent. Midfielders Adriano Moke, also 21, and Blackburn's 19 year old Michael Potts had also been signed, along with Lanre Oyebanjo, a fast-raiding full-back from Histon, also 21 years young, and things were looking rosy in Gary Mills garden.

Everybody at the club was full of optimism. Surely, surely this would be our year. We could feel it in our bones. The influx of young, promising players with pedigree would provide just the impetus we would need for a promotion push.

Honestly, I would rather have been in a better financial situation than I found myself in, but having lost my mother in February, and being restricted to a three-day contract, at a local supermarket, I knew that my away-days would sadly be limited this season.

So, it was left to the inimitable Barry Parker, and his sidekick Christopher Jones, erstwhile hero of the 1970s City side, to tell me all about proceedings, starting at Stonebridge Road, the home of Ebbsfleet United. Here we go again.

Five of the afore-mentioned new signings made their debut; Walker, Moke, Oyebanjo, McLaughlin and Blair. City defenders David McGurk and Chris Smith were both booked in the first half with the lively Enver-Marum causing problems with his pace. Ingham had to make a finger-tip save to deny the dangerous striker on the half hour mark. Matty Blair then showed his lightning speed, bursting through the home defence, but was denied by keeper Joe Welch's fingertips as he tried to dribble round him.

City stepped on the gas in the second half with full-backs Meredith and Oyebanjo risking bombing forward on the flanks. Boucaud had an exquisite curling shot which bounced off the underside of the bar, and it seemed (to most people at the ground), that it may have crossed the line. It wasn't given, and Boucaud was denied his long-awaited debut goal at this level.

The match erupted in the 69th minute after Fleet's Tom Phipp was dismissed for what seemed an innocuous challenge on Adriano Moke. The length of time the referee had taken to come to his decision had seemed to annoy the home supporters as much as anything.

City should have seized the initiative against the ten men, but Ebbsfleet's substitute Callum Willock turned the tables for the hosts just three minutes after entering the fray. According to the radio chaps he had somehow managed to beat Ingham to a cross, without impeding him, and headed the ball into the net. Having just been given a lucky break with the harsh red card for Phipp, the referee had seemed to have evened things up, and the goal was given in spite of massive protests from the City players. Here we go again, it was just typical of City's rotten luck.

City were down but they were far from out, and refused to accept defeat graciously. Ashley Chambers' blistering pace took him deep into the box, and as he rounded keeper Welch, his feet were taken from underneath him. Penalty.

Jason Walker coolly sidefooted the ball into the net to level the scores as Welch dived to his right. Redemption for the City striker after his misery in missing for the Hatters last time out in the play-off Final. City were right back in the hunt.

They stormed into the Ebbsfleet half like they were hungry for the victory, and this would set the scene for many encounters in the future months. In the second minute of added time, that man Walker rose above the Ebbsfleet keeper, and headed in the winner from eight yards out. Hallelujah, what a start to City's season. It was no more than they deserved but they had shown great spirit and fight to come back from being behind as late as the 83rd minute. That's just the kind of fighting spirit we would need to make those play-offs or better, by the end of April. A happy journey home, I gather.

EBBSFLEET UNITED: Welch, Stone, Simpemba, Easton, Herd, Phipp, Fakinos, (Stavrinou 66), Marwa, West, Shakes (Willock 76), Enver-Marum.

YORK CITY: Ingham, Oyebanjo, Meredith, Moke, McGurk, Smith, Boucaud, McLaughlin, Walker, Chambers, Blair.

Subs not used: Parslow, Reed, Potts, Fyfield, Henderson.

EBBSFLEET 1   CITY 2   Attendance: 1,522.

Scorers: EBBSFLEET, Willock 80   **CITY,** Walker 83 (pen 90+2).

CITY were up and running. Our first home game at the Crescent brought up a meeting with Jason Walkers old chums from Barrow, the club he left before he went to Luton. It was time to meet up with my small circle of friends to renew acquaintances after the close season.

Ted was well up for this one, and so was Bill. I had seen Ted a few times in the close season, and he was really upbeat about our chances this time out. Bootham was buzzing in anticipation.

The Barrow team included two ex-City players Adam Boyes and Andy Ferrell, plus a certain Gavin Skelton, a player who was well known to me. He had featured in the famous Gretna side who were promoted three seasons running, and ended up in the Scottish Premiership. Skelton had only missed 14 games out of Gretna's six year stint in the Scottish League. (But that is another story).

Jason Walker, still buzzing from his opening day brace was eager to carry on where he left off at Ebbsfleet. He was involved with everything right from the start. From a 7th minute corner, Walker flicked the ball back to Ashley Chambers who came steaming in, and flashed the ball against the post. Jason Walker eagerly gobbled up the rebound and we were celebrating our first home goal of the season, and Walker's third goal already.

It seemed that City had some new ingredients in their team. They were playing with a swagger; crisp, fast-flowing passing, and it was pleasing to the eye. Walker flashed another drive wide, then Matty Blair missed a couple of easy chances to put City further ahead.

In first half stoppage time, another one of City's many flowing moves provided their second goal. Meredith, on the left flank delivered an accurate pass to McLaughlin, who paused to control the ball, turned and swept it inside Hurst's left hand post.

I was astounded at the sheer pace of our new winger, Matty Blair. I remember an occasion early in the second half when he tore down the left flank leaving everybody in his wake. Sadly when he pulled the ball back for Walker he was unable to put the ball away. However that number 17 of ours was clearly going to cause a lot of problems running at Conference defenders this coming season for sure. I was well impressed with him.

Less impressed on 81 minutes, though. Wouldn't you just know it, our former striker Adam Boyes somehow managed to beat the City defence to get his header in and planted it past Michael Ingham to make it 2-1. How many times have we seen our ex-favourites doing that before?

City deserved their victory for their dominance throughout the game. They made it 3-1 when substitute Michael Potts dragged the ball back from the goal line for that man Blair to claim his first City goal as he sidefooted in from six yards, celebrating in front of us.

We were happy bunnies, having won two out of two so far. We were not too bothered about other teams results just yet; let's wait and see if we can win three out of three, and look at the "embryo" league table then.

YORK CITY: Ingham, Oyebanjo, Meredith, Moke (Potts 79), McGurk, Smith, Boucaud, McLaughlin, Walker (Reed 82), Chambers, Blair.

Subs not used: Parslow, Henderson, Fyfield.

BARROW: Hurst, Lomax, Bolland (Pearson), Quinn, Skelton, Smith, Sheridan (Cook), Ferrell, Almond (Mackreth), Boyes, Rutherford.

CITY 3   BARROW 1   Attendance: 3,075.

Scorers: CITY, Walker 7; McLaughlin 45+2; Blair 90+5   **BARROW,** Boyes 81.

Now it was the turn of AFC Telford to test out City's mettle; the team that City had despatched in the FA Trophy semi-finals 3 years earlier. They had one Craig Farrell in their ranks, but the ex-City striker was not in the starting line-up.

As usual, it was my chum Ted's duty to purchase my match day programme for me in case of my late arrival. Talk was whether or not City would be topping the table at 5 O'clock, we certainly hoped we would be.

It was a one-sided game, but with the wrong result from City's point of view. Oyebanjo fired high and wide with a long range effort on 25 minutes, then moments later Moke dragged a weak effort wide as well.

A free-kick by McLaughlin was also wasted, after Moke's flick header drifted past the post following a touch off Matty Blair.

In the seeond half it was all City once again. Oyebanjo hit the bar as the ball bounced up off his shins from a cross by Meredith. Chambers shot straight at keeper Young, then Jason Walker glanced a header wide from a McLaughlin corner. Next, City's new favourite saw his snap-shot going a foot wide of Young's right hand post. It was all City, but for all their pressure they just could not find the net.

On 84 minutes, that man Craig Farrell came on to replace Andy Brown. You might have bet on it. A couple of minutes later our ex-striker tucked away the rebound after Trainer hit the post, and City were one down with 4 minutes remaining. If ever there was a moment when I felt entitled to chuck my programme on the floor then this was it. I did not do that on this occasion. The old boys curse had come back to haunt City once again. How many more times, I wonder?

This time City's efforts at pulling back a goal failed miserably, and our dreams of topping the embryo table were history.

Meanwhile, in the Conference, Luton Town had hit their straps. They despatched Southport 5-1 at Kenilworth Road. Gateshead drew at home to Kettering, so City would have gone top with a win. Fleetwood and Wrexham, last seasons play-off semi-final losers joined Gateshead on 7 points following wins against Hayes and Yeading and Lincoln respectively. City were just behind in 5th position. Very early days yet.

YORK CITY: Ingham, Oyebanjo, Meredith, Moke (Fyfield 64), McGurk, Smith, Boucaud (Kerr 76), McLaughlin, Walker, Chambers, Blair (Reed 47). **Subs not used:** Parslow, Potts.

AFC TELFORD: Young, Salmon, Killock, Preston, Newton, King (Meechan), Trainer, Davies, Valentine, Reid (Samuels), Brown (Farrell).

CITY 0   TELFORD 1   **Attendance:** 2,723

Scorer: TELFORD, Farrell 86.

City needed to recover from what was considered an unfortunate and unexpected blip.

The blue-shirted warriors set about Kettering like a pack of hungry wolves after their prey. Their killer instinct was evident for all to see. Chris Smith headed wide from Ashley Chambers' cross after less than 45 seconds, and it was all just a blue haze for poor Kettering after that.

Andre Boucaud finally netted his first ever Conference goal on 20 minutes. Oyebanjo flicked it on to Walker, who in turn found Boucaud with a reverse pass and the Trinidadian midfielder slotted in past Lawrie Walker with the aplomb of a prolific striker.

Next a storming run by Moke down the left, just a minute later, produced a first time cross after Moke beat his man, and Walker converted to make it 2-0.

On the half hour, rampant City went 3 up. Oyebanjo hurled in a long throw, Smith headed on, and Walker was sharp enough to stick it away in an instant for his fifth goal in less than three and a half games.

Poor Kettering were in a spin. Boos were already ringing out from the Nene Park faithful. Another surging raid by City in the 39th minute caused the Poppies a lot more grief. Chambers did a one-two with Walker, and the ex-Luton man went tearing down the right before delivering an inch-perfect cross for Moke to come charging in and tap in City's fourth from close range. This was scintillating football, and it was happily becoming the "new" city team's trademark. They would soon be winning much acclaim for their classy, crisp and fast passing play this season.

Kettering pulled one back to make the half-time score 4-1 in City's favour. A cross by Moses Ashikodi eluded the City defence and McKenzie beat Ingham at his near post, in front of a totally empty goal-line stand.

Suffice to say that City coasted home in the end. Substitute Danny Pilkington came on to make his debut on 89 minutes, and still found time to find the net from 12 yards out after yet another surging run by Chambers, and more boos echoed from the mouths of home supporters.

Three wins out of four for City, and another happy journey home.

Wrexham had beaten Tamworth 3-0, Luton had drawn at Mansfield, and Fleetwood had surprisingly been trounced 4-0 at Barrow by Jason Walker's old chums. City were lying 3rd, a point behind the leaders.

KETTERING: L. Walker, Ifil (P), Ifil (J), Navarro, Clapham, Verma, Noubissie (Challinor), Marna, Kelly (Thomson), Ashikodi, McKenzie (Taft).

YORK CITY: Ingham, Oyebanjo, Meredith, Kerr, McGurk, Smith, Boucaud, McLaughlin(Reed 54), Walker (Pilkington 89), Chambers, Moke (Fyfield 79).

Subs not used: Parslow, Potts.

KETTERING 1   CITY 5   Attendance: 1,595.

Scorers: KETTERING, McKenzie 43   **CITY,** Boucaud 20; Walker 21, 30; Moke 39; Pilkington 90+4.

Next up, City faced a trip to Highbury on a Friday night. No, not THAT Highbury, you understand, the more humble home of Fleetwood Town instead. They had reacted from a surprise thrashing at Barrow by forking out 100 grand for the services of Jamie Vardy from FC Halifax. City, for their part, had secured the services of Jon Challinor from Kettering, whom City had put to the sword 3 days earlier. That "Angel of the North" would also be facing City, name of Richard Brodie. Evidently, City would have their work cut out from keeping Messrs Vardy and Brodie off the scoresheet, it would be a severe test of City's credentials in defence.

The match was screened live on Premier Sports TV. It was a typical gritty Battle of the Roses throughout. Fair to say that Fleetwood had the best of chances, but City had their moments too.

Brodie's early free kick stung the hands of Michael Ingham but he held on easily. McLaughlin headed straight into the Fleetwood keeper's hands, then headed another harmlessly wide. City had the best chance of the first half. Jason Walker flicked the ball on to Chambers who was hurtling down the right flank like Usain Bolt. Chambers ran on, and should have given Davies a shot to save, instead he curled it wide of the keeper's right hand post. Goalless at half-time.

Fleetwood took command early in the second half. Harvey missed a golden chance from 8 yards out, then the dangerous Brodie tested Ingham once again, but his shot had no power or direction.

New signing Vardy was getting used to the pace at Conference level, first he pulled an angled shot well wide, and then whipped over a cross which Brodie headed over at the far post. So far so good. As long as Brodie did not score, that's what some City fans were thinking. As long as Fleetwood didn't score, that's what I was thinking.

Actually City could have won it in the dying minutes. Dave McGurk stole in at the far post and nicked the ball wide from 5 yards out, just getting his toe to the ball before the Fleetwood defence.

There was one more moment of worry for City yet to come, as once again Brodie forced Ingham into a useful save, but the ball broke free to Alex-Ray Harvey who fired in a piledriver which once again stung Ingham's hands, but City survived.

This result had more than pleased City manager Gary Mills. Fleetwood were always going to be front-runners for the title with the likes of Brodie, Vardy and Magno Vieira in a three-pronged attack, with money in the coffers for manager Mellon to shore up his defence. City had proved that they were not only a dangerous attacking unit as well as Fleetwood, but they could also adapt to a situation where they had to be more resolute at the back as well. A very useful point indeed, at this early stage of the season. City were still unbeaten on the road.

On Saturday Wrexham won easily at Alfreton, and Luton Town were ominously heading for the top six with a comfortable 3-1 win at home to Braintree. Wrexham were top, with Gateshead, having won at Barrow, second, and City were third, together with Kidderminster and Tamworth, three points off the top.

FLEETWOOD: Davies, Brown (Milligan 83), McNulty, Atkinson, Edwards, Holmes, McGuire, Harvey, Vardy, Brodie, Vieira.

YORK CITY: Ingham, Oyebanjo, Meredith, Kerr, McGurk, Smith, Boucaud (Fyfield 78), McLaughlin (Challinor 56), Walker, Chambers, Moke (Pilkington 62).

Subs not used: Parslow, Reed.

FLEETWOOD 0   CITY 0   Attendance: 2,111.

ALFRETON Town were our next opponents at the Crescent on Bank Holiday Monday, August 29th. The Derbyshire outfit, having just won the Conference North Title by a clear 10 points were struggling at the higher level, and were bottom of the table having gleaned a meagre 2 points from their first 5 games.

Football fans are a strange breed. When you are a supporter of York City, you can take absolutely nothing for granted I assure you. Some of my City pals were dreaming of an easy victory to put us firmly ensconced in the early play-off places by 5 O'clock that night. The smart money was on a comfortable City victory.

Alfreton included two more ex-City men, one Levi Mackin, who had featured in City's play off defeat at Wembley in 2010, and Greg Young, a centre back who didn't really do himself justice at City during the previous season. Surely there would be no case of old boys putting one past City once again. Adam Boyes and Craig Farrell had already done just that this season.

With just 3 minutes on the clock, Ashley Chambers was up to his tricks again, but having outpaced his marker once again he sliced a clear chance horribly wide. Danny Parslow celebrated his return to the side with a 30 yard drive which flew well over the bar.

Next up, the brilliant McLaughlin collected a long ball from Boucaud, beat the challenge of Greg Young easily, but the keeper managed to keep out the Irishman's shot with his outstretched leg. The chances kept on coming for the Minstermen. Walker had a close range effort scrambled away by the Alfreton defence, and Meredith shot weakly at the visiting keeper.

City were made to pay for their missed chances on 42 minutes. Andre Boucaud, in the corner of City's box made a clumsy tackle on Paul Clayton and there was no doubt it was a clear penalty.

Surprise of all surprises, up stepped Levi Mackin to take the kick. A more unlikely scorer you could hardly imagine. The Welshman had only netted once for City in 67 appearances. Here we go again.

Mackin became the third ex-City player to score against his former club, as he calmly slotted the ball inside Ingham's left hand post. 1-0 to the minnows from Derbyshire.

Alfreton had the spirit and desire to do what they do best. They blocked and tackled every time the Minstermen threatened, and they hung on to their precious lead. Even when Jamie Reed came on for Paddy McLaughlin at half-time they failed to penetrate Alfreton's ranks. Headers from both Reed and Walker were easily saved, and Scotty Kerr shot high and wide. Finally in the dying moments, Moke danced into the box, shimmied left, and beat his man, then fired straight into the grateful keeper's tender areas ! Chambers had a long shot saved in stoppage time, and that was that. City had suffered back to back home defeats and I for one, was beginning to wonder just how good or bad they really were.

August ended with 10 points out of 18, with 7 of them coming away from the Crescent. They were 6th in the Blue Square Conference.

Wrexham had won a ding-dong battle 2-0 against Fleetwood at the Racecourse, and Gateshead had despatched Grimsby 1-0 at home. Luton drew 2-2 at Hayes on Tuesday evening.

YORK CITY: Ingham, Parslow, Meredith (Fyfield 63), Kerr, McGurk, Smith, Boucaud (Challinor 57), McLaughlin (Reed 46), Walker, Chambers, Moke.

Sub not used: Pilkington and Potts.

ALFRETON: Lowson, Franks, Wilson, Young, Franklin, Mullan, Streete, Mackin, Brown, Clayton (Jarman 83), Senior (Ellison 89).

CITY 0   ALFRETON 1   Attendance: 3,166.

Scorer: ALFRETON, Mackin (pen) 43.

BLUE SQUARE CONFERENCE TABLE
AT AUGUST 31, 2011 (TOP 10)

1.	Wrexham	6	5	1	0	14-3	16
2.	Gateshead	6	5	1	0	13-5	16
3.	Kidderminster	6	4	1	1	11-6	13
4.	Darlington	6	3	2	1	7-4	11
5.	Tamworth	6	3	2	1	7-6	11
6.	YORK CITY	6	3	1	2	10-5	10
7.	Forest Gn	6	2	3	1	12-6	9
8.	Luton T	5	2	3	0	12-6	9
9.	Cambridge	6	2	2	2	6-6	8
10.	Fleetwood	6	2	2	2	3-6	8

CHAPTER 4
SEPTEMBER: MAKE OR BREAK

THE FIRST Saturday of September arrived with City having no game. Three of their players were absent due to International commitments. Andre Boucaud had joined the Trinidad and Tobago squad for World Cup Qualifiers. Patrick McLaughlin was on duty with Northern Ireland under 21s, and Lanre Oyebanjo was with the Republic of Ireland under-21 squad.

Instead I was glued to my computer watching the Conference results unfold. It wasn't happy viewing, I can tell you. Wrexham, Gateshead, Mansfield and Fleetwood all won, and Luton would have won at Stockport but for a late equaliser by County which was the only joy I managed to obtain during the afternoon. The two late goals by Kettering were not enough to halt Fleetwood's march as they came out 3-2 winners and went up to 8th spot.

It all left City floundering in 10th position with a game in hand, 9 points off the top, and a point below the play-off positions.

Off we went to Tamworth next. Gary Mills old club had thwarted City's bid for the play-offs last season, scuppering our hopes with a 2-1 win at the Crescent. Wouldn't you just know it but former City man Ben Wilkinson had scored Tamworth's opener on that day.

It was a blustery old day at the "Lamb" ground, and City hoped they would not become "Lambs to the slaughter". Boucaud and Oyebanjo were back from International duty, with Paddy McLaughlin. Of the three, Oyebanjo played in the right back slot, and the other two were rested. Jon Challinor started for the first time, on the right flank, and Matty Blair returned after a 3-game absence.

Tamworth had by far the better chances in the first period, as City's passing game seemed to have gone missing, after their 12 days of inertia. Nabil Shariff headed wide from a Jay Smith free-kick, as Tamworth pressed deep into City's territory. The visitors first real chance came midway through the half. A speculative 35 yarder by Challinor failed to trouble the Tamworth keeper.

Jason Walker scuffed his shot wide, and Challinor came dashing in at the far post and crashed the ball into the side netting. Tamworth came back, and Mills shot narrowly wide, then Daniel Bradley's shot was cleared away by Chris Smith, on his return to his former home.

Things got worse for City's skipper on his return to the Lamb. On 52 minutes the City captain was, slightly harshly penalised for having his arms around Keiron St Aimie's shoulders, and pulling him back. The Tamworth striker took the penalty himself, planting the ball inside Ingham's right hand post in front of the disappointed City fans.

Next, the unfortunate City captain bumped into Danny Thomas, and he got no benefit of any doubt from referee Graham Horwood who had no hesitation in pointing to the spot again. Same result, only this time Iyseden Christie rifled the ball into the roof of Ingham's net and City were 2-0 down.

Six minutes from time, Jason Walker rose majestically to meet a delicious cross from Chambers, and head the ball firmly past Jonathan Hedge to give City a lifeline. Could they come back from the dead?

Tamworth fans were audibly annoyed with the amount of stoppage time being played. Fully six minutes into the added period came City's last salvo, and it came from substitute McLaughlin who thumped in a half-volley which the keeper managed to push safely over the bar, and now City's unbeaten record on the road had gone.

City were really struggling now, in 14th position, and in the bottom half of the table for the first time since November 2010 and it wasn't very nice to look at the League Table on September 11.

Gateshead went down at Fleetwood, and Wrexham went down at Barrow. Luton beat Darlington 2-0, and the form team Mansfield slapped Newport, 5-0 to go 3rd. Tamworth were up to 5th, with Fleetwood and Luton lurking just below them. City were 9 points off the top.

TAMWORTH: Hedge, Tait, Francis, Green, Habergham, Shariff (Cain 83), Bradley, Jay Smith, Mills (Christie 68), St Aimie, Patterson (Thomas 28).

YORK CITY: Ingham, Oyebanjo, Meredith, Kerr, McGurk, Chris Smith, Challinor (Henderson 66), Moke (Reed 46), Walker, Chambers, Blair (McLaughlin 54).

Subs not used: Parslow, Boucaud.

TAMWORTH 2   CITY 1   **Attendance:** 1,012.

Scorers: TAMWORTH, St Aimie (pen) 53; Christie (pen) 73   **CITY,** Walker 84.

CITY simply had to bounce back in their next game at home to Bath City, the re-arranged fixture from 10 days earlier. This time, Bath were bottom of the table, and we all hoped to perform a good deal better than we had done the last time we had played the bottom side.

Nobody was predicting anything this time. Not after the Alfreton debacle.

Jamal Fyfield came in for Smithy after his nightmare at his former club. Andre Boucaud returned to his midfield spot, and Danny Parslow replaced the injured Oyebanjo. Pilkington started for the first time.

Surprisingly, Bath City were a lively outfit, considering they had only netted three times in seven outings. First, Ingham saved a 25-yarder from Swallow, and then had to be at full stretch to tip a dangerous header from Phillips over his bar. City were giving the ball away far too easily for my liking, and the visitors were visibly growing in confidence.

Chambers scuffed wide after half an hour, City's first real chance, then Fyfield headed over from a corner. At last, we were on the move.

In the first minute of first half stoppage time, Jon Challinor was scythed down in full flow by Charlie Clough. Sadly, Jason Walker's debut penalty at the Crescent went sailing over the bar and into the visitors enclosure.

In the second half, City laboured on. In the last 2 games, Reedy had come on at half-time to beef up the City attack. This time he was left to fester on the bench until the last 5 minutes. One memory of City's early season pass and move game returned when Meredith, Boucaud, and Chambers combined to provide a chance for Walker, who came hurtling in at the far post but saw his shot easily saved.

Suddenly, Bath's Ben Swallow burst clear of the City defence on 75 minutes, chasing after a through ball. Michael Ingham brought him down, and that was that. Miraculously, the City keeper made amends by diving full length to his left and saved Swallow's effort to keep us in the game.

Reedy duly came on to replace Chambers in the dying minutes. Once again our "Supersub" was left to pull City out of the mire. A mere 3 minutes after he came on, the ball was whipped across from a City corner, Jason Walker flicked it on to the far post. Somehow the ball found its way to Reedy, lurking on the six-yard line, and he gobbled up the chance with glee.

Thanks to "Supersub" we did it again. Some would say a lucky win, but there you are. That's the value of having a good squad of players I suppose. Nobody was complaining. Nobody in the Longhurst Stand at any rate. City were up to 9th.

YORK CITY: Ingham, Parslow, Meredith, Kerr, McGurk, Fyfield, Challinor (Henderson 69), Boucaud, Walker, Chambers (Reed 85), Pilkington (Blair 74)

Subs not used: Smith, McLaughlin.

BATH CITY: Garner, Simpson, Jones, Clough, Stonehouse, Watkins, Burnell, Canham, Connolly, Swallow (Egan), Phillips (Preece).

CITY 1 BATH 0   **Attendance**: 2,030.

Scorer: CITY, Reed 88.

Now for another Real test, of City's ability. The victory over Bath was unconvincing to put it mildly. Wrexham were flying high at the top of the table, unbeaten at their Racecourse Ground.

City were out of the traps from minute one. They meant business now. Ingham made a comfortable save from a Pogba volley, and then the Minstermen went on the rampage. Jason Walker was bundled to the ground by Nat Knight-Percival, and City shaped up for the set-piece.

Paddy McLaughlin played a one-two with Ashley Chambers, then unleashed a delicious shot straight into the top corner of young Mayebi's net. One-up after just 4 minutes.

This was just the boost to City's confidence that they needed. Walker came close with a couple of efforts, then Andre Boucaud set up Reedy whose shot was comfortably saved. City were, rampant now, and the wave after wave of attacks by the blue-clad Minstermen continued. It was all City now.

Jason Walker headed on an Ingham clearance, and Chambers latched on to it like a cobra and before the Dragon's defence had time to blink, he ran on and lobbed the oncoming keeper to put City two-up after 21 minutes.

Promoted from his super-sub role, to making his first start of the season, Reedy wanted to make the most of his chance. A typical fast moving passing build up finished up with the ball at Reedy's feet, with his back to goal. He turned, beat his man, and beat the keeper in the blink of an eye. It was a typical striker's opportunist goal and it put City three up against the League-leaders, and surely out of sight.

It seemed just like an exhibition match or something, the way that City had re-discovered their game of controlled passing and movement, so much so that Wrexham hardly got a piece of the action. City were back in their stride, and how.

City seemed content to sit back and defend their lead. To be honest, they were never greatly troubled by Wrexham's best endeavours, although Ingham was the busier keeper in the second period. Weak shots by Keates and Pogba were easily gathered by the City keeper, and even when Jake Speight was bearing down upon his goal, he managed to smother the ball as well.

Substitute Michael Potts could have made it four, moments before the end. His dipping shot sailed just over the bar, below the celebrating City faithful. That would just have been too unfair on Wrexham.

City had proved that they were back to form. New skipper Scott Kerr was like a little General in midfield, guiding and inspiring his men, and getting in the way of Wrexham's sporadic surges forward. Jamal Fyfield and Dave McGurk were comfortable at the back, and Gary Mills must have been delighted with the performance of his team. Not many would come away from here with three points in the bag.

Meanwhile, in the Conference, Luton Town were giving City fans a lot to be alarmed about. They had leapt up to second in the table after a win over Lincoln, and were looking hot. Fleetwood won again, at Ebbsfleet, and were 7th, one place above City, who found ourselves just a single point off the play-off spots. Things were looking brighter once again. Consistency is what we needed now.

WREXHAM: Mayebi, Obeng, Westwood, Knight-Percival, Ashton, Harris, Fowler, Tolley (Cieslewicz), Morrell (Keates), Pogba, Speight.

YORK CITY: Ingham, Challinor, Meredith, Kerr, McGurk, Fyfield, Boucaud (Potts 66), McLaughlin, Walker, Chambers, Reed (Blair 66).

Subs not used: Smith, Parslow, Henderson.

WREXHAM 0   CITY 3   Attendance: 3,872.

Scorers: CITY, McLaughlin 4; Chambers 21; Reed 24.

DARLINGTON came down the A1 for a good old-fashioned local Derby battle with City. They were having a fairly decent season with 12 points in 9 games, in a comfortable mid-table position. Local Derbies are never easy. The Quakers had former City full-back Ben Purkiss in their side. Wonder what the odds against him scoring were.

Reedy kept his place, in what seemed like a 4-3-3 set up once again. This had proved effective at Wrexham, and it was soon to pay dividends early on.

A raking through ball from Chambers in the second minute saw Walker flick on to the path of Reedy. Like the predator that he is, the popular ex-Bangor man latched on to it in a flash and despatched an unstoppable shot past Sam Russell. City were up and running after a mere 65 seconds, and the "Shippo" was jubilant.

City were looking comfortable, and in full control, until a lapse occurred in their defensive ranks. The unflappable Dave McGurk allowed the ball to slip through him, leaving James Walshaw to run on and round Ingham with ease to plant the ball into an empty net for the Darlington equaliser.

Things got worse on the half-hour mark. A cross by former City favourite Ben Purkiss flicked off Fyfield's head, and flew across the box. Reedy was adjudged to have pushed Adam Rundle, and referee Wiggleworth pointed to the spot. Bridge-Wilkinson's penalty was rifled into Ingham's net as the keeper dived to the left. For all City's early confidence we were one down to our local rivals, and that's the way it stayed till the half-time whistle blew.

Undismayed, City's fighting spirit came back strong after the interval, as they surged towards their Shippo faithful. Reedy raced on to an Ingham clearance, but his shot finished wide of Russell's post.

McLaughlin missed a couple of speculative 20-yard shots, then another shot by Walker, following a Chambers free-kick was saved by Russell. Chances were going begging, as time was running out. The City faithful needed a bit of magic to cheer them up.

We got it in the 79th minute, and what an exquisite goal it was as well. That star man Jason Walker was having a golden season. He found himself, at the left edge of the penalty box, not far from the goal line. He checked his stride, cut inside, and unleashed a curler straight into the top right stanchion, out of reach of the keeper's despairing dive, and the "Shippo" went ballistic.

Searching for a winner came to nothing. Darlington had been a lively outfit and possibly, grudgingly deserved a draw. A draw is better than a defeat. It wasn't enough, but it would have to do with Luton coming next.

The Hatters had also drawn, at Bath, and they were sitting ominously, on top of the pile, but only 3 points ahead of City. Fleetwood, having despatched Kidderminster 5-2 were looming large in 4th place now, level with Wrexham, who also drew, at Southport, and Gateshead, who went down at Lincoln. All the afore-mentioned clubs had 20 points, and City were 3 points behind in 7th place. NOW FOR THE BIG ONE on September 24th.

YORK CITY: Ingham, Challinor, Meredith, Kerr, McGurk, Fyfield, Boucaud (Moke 77), McLaughlin, Walker, Chambers, Reed.

Subs not used: Parslow, Henderson, Potts, Blair.

DARLINGTON: Russell, Purkiss, Lee, Miller, Brown (Brough), Chandler, Taylor, Bridge-Wilkinson, Rundle, Purcell (Hatch), Walshaw (Bowman).

CITY 2   DARLINGTON 2   **Attendance:** 2,834.

Scorers: CITY, Reed 2; Walker 79.   **DARLINGTON,** Walshaw 10; Bridge-Wilkinson (pen) 31.

THIS WAS IT. This was the big one, in every sense of the word. September 24 was the biggest date on any City fan's calendar so far this season.

Luton Town are City's nemesis and our sworn enemies. Or is that the wrong way around. All of City's fans they know the history. Suffice to say that the events of May the 3rd, 2010 are well documented elsewhere, and the happenings of that sad day in Conference football will never be forgotten by the City faithful who were there. Ask my (then) ten year old nephew about it and he will be brought to tears by the memory of it all.

The Hatters had beaten City once, and once only in our six meetings since they were dumped into the Conference. (A 5-0 thrashing after Ingham got his marching orders). City had beaten Luton 1-0 at home last season, drawn with them twice on the previous campaign, and, of course, despatched them from the play-offs, courtesy of Brodie and Carruthers, but all that was History now.

Eager with the anticipation of it all, I set off a few minutes earlier than normal, to enjoy the pre-match atmosphere, and have a chat with my chums.

Such is the nature of football at this level, that I often find myself chatting with visiting supporters before a game. I would not chat to Luton fans for reasons which should be obvious.

Strolling past the visitor's end before the game, I noticed a group of Orange clad supporters laughing and joking as they entered the ground.

I walked sedately past them, unperturbed, and not wishing to involve myself in conversation. I saw a Steward whose face I vaguely knew and I carefully whispered in his ear.

"They won't be laughing at five O'clock ! !! "

And they weren't.

Everyone was full of it. City fans and players alike knew that if we beat the Hatters by 2 clear goals we would be above them in the table. That was all that mattered at this early stage of the season, really.

Inside, the ground was buzzing. Of the players on duty in the 2010 play-offs, only Michael Ingham, James Meredith, Dave

McGurk, and Danny Parslow remained on City's books. Alex Lawless had played for City then, but had defected to the Hatters, believing that they had a better chance of going up. Jason Walker had joined the Hatters early in 2011 and had not figured in their 2010 defeat. He had not really settled at Kenilworth Road, and made the wise choice of joining City in the summer.

City were well up for this one. They were rampant from the start. In the ninth minute, Jason Walker rose high above his marker. Paddy McLaughlin then released Chambers, who cut inside, and unleashed a sumptuous curler in from just outside the box, way beyond the desperate dive of keeper Mark Tyler. It was an exquisite moment, and it sent the City faithful into raptures.

But that was just a starter course. The main course was yet to come. On the half hour mark, Kerr fed Chambers down the left, and the ball came to Reedy, who eventually scrambled the ball from underneath his feet before feeding Walker who drilled a 15-yard first time drive into the net off Tyler's left hand post. Delirium ensued.

"There's only one Jason Walker" echoed from the mouths of Shippo-ites. Luton were deflated. More than that, they were a beaten side. The more they taunted Mr Walker, the more of a danger he would become to Luton, and they realised that.

Luton for their part had a few chances but nothing really threatening. Stuart Fleetwood almost cleared the Shippo roof with a wild effort, then went closer with a snap-shot which flashed just wide.

In the second minute of added first half time a poor Luton clearance fell to that man Walker, he crossed it first time and Ashley Chambers hurtled in to volley into the net for his second of the game, and City's third. YORK CITY 3, LUTON TOWN 0. How good was that for City's faithful. You can bet it was the best feeling in the world.

Alex Lawless failed to appear for the second half. He was injured, apparently. Some sources said that his fist had had an argument with the dressing room door. Ah well.

Ashley Chambers should have claimed his hat-trick in the first minute of the second half. He shot a foot wide from 20 yards out.

Luton's Jamie Hand blasted over from eight yards after a lapse in City's concentration. But, we were coasting to victory now.

Jason Walker unleashed an astonishing lob from 35 yards which had Tyler scrambling after it, only to see the ball bounce off the crossbar. Luton had their chances but failed to put any of them away. Ingham saved from Howells, and Kovak's header failed to find the net as well. Keane's final effort was also saved by Ingham.

Right at the death, a City free kick by McLaughlin sailed over the bar and into the Shippo end, and then the final whistle blew.

So, Luton had gone the same way as Wrexham, and City were well and truly, back on the right track. The best thing was that Luton were below City on goal-difference now, the Minstermen in 5th place (in the play-off slots), and Luton sixth. Wrexham won at Grimsby, and remained top, Gateshead were 2nd having won at Hayes, and Fleetwood snatched a late draw at home to Telford to stay in 4th. Gateshead were our next opponents.

Everyone at Bootham Crescent was very happy. The Luton fans who were laughing at half past two were not laughing now.

YORK CITY: Ingham, Challinor, Meredith, Kerr, McGurk, Fyfield, Boucaud, McLaughlin, Walker (Henderson 90), Chambers (Blair 76), Reed (Moke 66). **Subs not used:** Smith, Parslow.

LUTON TOWN: Tyler, Keane, Kovaks, Antwi, Howells, Kissock, (O'Connor), Lawless (Watkins), Hand, Dance, Fleetwood (Crow), Wilmott.

CITY 3   LUTON 0   **Attendance:** 3,570.

Scorers: CITY, Chambers 9, 45; Walker 31.

Ashley Chambers puts York 3-0 up against Luton at Bootham Crescent.
(Picture The Press, York).

Now, another tough trip, this time to the North-east beckoned, against another top side, Gateshead.

I was in the warehouse at the local Supermarket, when Faye summoned me over for a word.

"Do you fancy a trip to Gateshead this evening."

You bet I did.

It was a sunny Autumn afternoon as we hit the A1 North, full of hope that we had turned the corner, and found our consistency at last. Graham's girlfriend did the driving as he himself had just finished a 12 hour shift, or something like that.

At the Gateshead International Stadium you need a telescope to see the action properly. No matter, the 525 City fans out of a total "crowd" of 1,604 were far from bothered about things like that.

Yet another ex-City striker lined up against the Minstermen. Jon Shaw was already heading the Conference scoring charts with 10 league goals to date. Our own Jason Walker had notched 8 so far, so the match was dubbed as a battle between those two. We all know that there was more to it than that.

The "Heed" were taking no prisoners. Wouldn't you just know it, that fellow Shaw stole in un-marked on the six-yard line, was given a free header, and gratefully planted it into the net inside 3 minutes before City had time to catch their breath. Ouch.

It was all Gateshead, from what I could see from several miles away from the action! Cummins and Shaw missed further chances before the dangerous and muscular Odubade shot straight at Ingham.

However, City's first real attack on 23 minutes paid dividends. Reedy headed the ball through to Walker, who dinked a delightful little lob over keeper Farman, and we were (probably) undeservedly level. But not for long.

Just four minutes later a wicked cross from the right came arrowing towards the head of John Shaw. From an identical position to where he opened the scoring, he planted the ball in Ingham's net again for his 12th goal of the season. He never scored a single goal for City in his 8 appearances for the Minstermen!

Things went from bad to worse for City. Dave McGurk was caught flat-footed as Odubade came charging in at speed. The former Oxford striker had his shot saved, but the referee called play back and gave a free-kick anyway. Nothing came of it.

City's chances were few and far between. Boucaud dragged a rare shot wide of Farman's goal.

But Gateshead looked a useful outfit. Gillies and Cummins had further chances, and kept on dominating proceedings as they had done in the first half. The lively Odubade was grabbed at by Challinor as he was beaten for pace, and City had conceded their 6th penalty in 7 games. Shaw made no mistake, and slotted inside Ingham's left hand post to claim his second hat-trick in successive games. He had 13 goals to Walker's 9 by now.

Still City refused to lie down and surrender, with 2 minutes remaining they had a corner on the right which Moke delivered into the six-yard box. The unfortunate James Curtis got to the ball first, but planted it into his own net to keep City in the hunt, but only just.

City stormed ahead in a grandstand finish, with Blair shooting straight at Farman, and then Meredith clattered into the post as he tried to steer in a cross from Moke in the dying seconds, but it was all in vain. Gateshead 3, City 2. Nobody could complain too much.

The journey home was short, if not so sweet. Graham's girlfriend located the Burger Bar, and did the driving once again.

Fleetwood won at Stockport, and Mansfield had won at Wrexham. The only happy news that night was Cambridge beating Luton at their place, keeping City still ahead of the Hatters, but we were back down in 8th place now. Gateshead were top, and looking a good bet for promotion with that fellow Shaw in their squad.

GATESHEAD: Farman, Odhiambo, Curtis, Clark, Rents, Turnbull, Gate (Nix), Cummins, Odubade, Shaw, Gillies (Mulligan).

YORK CITY: Ingham, Challinor, Meredith, Kerr, McGurk, Fyfield, Boucaud, McLaughlin (Moke 65), Walker, Chambers (Henderson 70), Reed (Blair 46).

Subs not used: Smith, Parslow.

GATESHEAD 3   CITY 2   Attendance: 1,604.

Scorers: GATESHEAD, Shaw 3, 27 (pen), 68.   **CITY,** Walker, 23; Curtis (OG) 88.

BLUE SQUARE CONFERENCE TABLE
AT 30 SEPTEMBER 2011 (TOP 10)

1.	Gateshead	12	8	2	2	23-14	26
2.	Braintree T	12	8	1	3	23-10	25
3.	Fleetwood T	12	7	3	2	23-16	24
4.	Wrexham	12	7	2	3	21-13	23
5.	Mansfield	12	6	4	2	21-13	22
6.	Cambridge	12	6	4	2	14-8	22
7.	Kidderminster	12	6	3	3	22-17	21
8.	YORK CITY	12	6	2	4	22-12	20
9.	Luton Town	12	5	5	2	19-12	20
10.	Tamworth	12	5	3	4	13-13	18

CHAPTER 5
OCTOBER: THE WONDER OF WALKER

WITH teams like Stockport County, you never know just how they will adjust to non-league football after being relegated to the National Conference for the first time in their history. County had drawn no less than 8 of their first 12 games at this level, so far, including all 6 of their away games to date.

Jason Walker had netted 9 goals in City's first 12 games, and should he score at Edgeley Park he would beat the record for being the earliest ever marksman for City to make it 10.

It was a quiet first half, really. That man Walker had a chance early on, but the angle was too tight to pull it back to score. Then City had a sniff of a penalty on 22 minutes when Joe Edwards seemed to push the City marksman in the back, but nothing was given.

Walker actually did put the ball in the net in the very next minute, but this time he himself was adjudged to have pushed keeper Glennon in the back, ironically. Seemed like he was destined not to beat that record.

Meredith had a chance for City, but his shot was deflected wide, and County had their first attempt on 35 minutes when Chadwick headed over.

City upped the pace from the start of the second period. Substitute Michael Potts crossed to Walker on the left, and the City number 9 crossed for Matty Blair, who came hurtling in to head past Glennon. City were in charge.

Chadwick missed another header, and it wasn't long before he was taken off in favour of Tom Elliott, mainly due to cat-calls from the County fans, according to the radio. Stockport were a decent passing side but they were wasting the few chances they were making.

City made them pay for that with 4 minutes to go. Just when it seemed like Arthur Bottom and Jimmy Weir's records would still stand, it was Jason Walker who finally claimed that record for himself. Matty Blair went tearing down the right, and Walker charged into the box to meet his cross, and beat the keeper from 6 yards to put the ball in the net. He had beaten the old record by just one day, to score his 10th goal of the season.

That really should have been that but City switched off deep into injury time as their defence allowed Michael Paton a free header which he planted inside Ingham's right hand post to make it Stockport 1, City 2. That was good enough for me. Four away wins out of seven.

City moved up one position, or to be correct, they were 6th equal with Luton on points, and goal difference, and even goals scored. The Hatters had thrashed Barrow 5-1 at home. Wrexham squeezed a 1-0 win over Ebbsfleet, and Fleetwood won at Braintree, who were City's next opponents. Gateshead held onto top spot with a draw at home to Tamworth.

STOCKPORT COUNTY: Glennon, Edwards, Brahim-Bounab, Piergianni, Holden, Paton, Miles (Whitehead), Blackburn (Sheridan), Nolan, German, Chadwick (Elliott).

YORK CITY: Ingham, Challinor, Meredith, Kerr, Smith, Fyield, Boucaud (Potts 39), McLaughlin (Parslow 74), Walker, Chambers, Blair.

Subs not used: Reed, Henderson, Moke.

STOCKPORT 1   CITY 2   Attendance: 3,753.

Scorers: STOCKPORT, Paton 90+4.   **CITY,** Blair 52; Walker 86.

OCTOBER had started well for City. Another win and we could nudge into the play-off spot. City had lost at home to last season's Conference North Champions, and now it was the turn of

Braintree Town, the Southern Champions to meet City for the first time. The Essex boys had started surprisingly well in the Conference, and were standing 4th, just 2 points ahead of City on the morning of October 8.

City were unchanged from their trip to Stockport County. Once again they were unsure what to make of their opponents. Needless to say, the Minstermen had the upper hand, once they had survived an early scare when Braintree's Sean Marks headed over from an early free-kick.

On 15 minutes, Chambers surged down the right, collected a perfect pass from McLaughlin, cut inside his marker, and poked the ball into the net, as the keeper came rushing out. City were on their way.

Jason Walker volleyed wide, then Chambers tried a cheeky lob which the keeper managed to hold on to. Next, it was Meredith's turn to feel unlucky, as a last-ditch tackle prevented him getting a shot on goal. City were meaning business now.

Just, before the half hour mark, Meredith charged into the box, and released McLaughlin who rifled in a low shot, past the helpless Nathan McDonald. City were 2-up and they were going for the kill. Jamal Fyfield had kept his place alongside Smith, having taken Dave McGurk's place at Stockport due to McGurk's suspension. Matty Blair somehow kept the ball from going out, and hooked it across the goal where Jamal was lurking. In a flash he back-heeled the ball into the net, and celebrated like he had just won the World Cup, or the like. City 3, Braintree 0.

Still, City were not finished yet. Just 4 minutes later Walker passed to McLaughlin, who jumped over a lunging tackle, then drilled an unstoppable shot inside the keeper's near post. This was fast becoming a total rout. Seemed like Braintree's bubble had burst.

In a rare lapse on City's part, they allowed Sean Marks far too much space to latch on to a loose ball after a shot by Kenny Davis came back off the post. No matter, it was City 4, Braintree 1 at the interval, and surely that was quite enough for City to rise above the Essex boys in the table, at the end of the day.

It is probably, fair to say that City were coasting just a little on the hour. Braintree reminded the Minstermen that they were not completely out of the game just yet. Defender Aswad Thomas beat Ingham to his left from ten yards out to make it 4-2 to the Reds. On came Danny Parslow to ensure City had a little more defensive cover. They really did not need to be so negative, if truth be told. Five minutes after Parslow's introduction, City regained their 3-goal lead. Matty Blair was clearly dragged down in full flow by Dave Stevens, and the penalty was given, with the unlucky defender receiving his marching orders. Walker tucked the spot kick in the keeper's left corner as he unfortunately dived to the right. City were 5-2 up, and had a man advantage. They had yet to net 6 goals in the Conference.

Adriano Moke soon changed that. He replaced Chambers with 10 minutes to go, and enjoyed his escapades up and down the left flank in the short time remaining. With 5 minutes left on the clock, he scored what, in my opinion was City's best goal of the season yet. He set off on a mazy run as far as the edge of the penalty area, paused, and then composed himself, and curled an exquisite looping shot beyond the dive of Nathan McDonald. It was an exquisite goal to cap an exquisite display by City. It was the first time they had scored 6 in the Conference, and the first time they had netted 6 in a league game for 26 years. That goal would have done our Clayton Donaldson proud !

Braintree were down to 9 men for the last few seconds.Substitute Andy Yiadom received his marching orders for a dangerous airborne challenge on Chris Smith. It didn't matter a real lot. The final whistle sounded before he reached the dressing room.

This was time for celebrating. The Shippo End, the Pop Stand, and, the Main Stand customers roared the City heroes off the pitch.

My own celebrations were far from extravagant. This, I decided was the time for me to tuck into my favourite meal when I got home. It was time for me to go and get my fish and chips ! ! !

So it was that City moved up to 4th, and we had made the play-off zone at last. Luton had done us a favour by beating Kidderminster at their place, but City now headed the Hatters on goal difference. Gateshead scraped a 1-0 win at Ebbsfleet, Fleetwood were surprisingly held at home by Forest Green, and were 3rd, two points ahead of City. Those fish and chips were good.

YORK CITY: Ingham, Challinor, Meredith, Kerr, Smith, Fyfield, Boucaud (Parslow 67), McLaughlin, Walker (Reed 86), Chambers (Moke 79) Blair.

Subs not used: McGurk, Potts.

BRAINTREE TOWN: McDonald, O'Connor, Bailey-Dennis, Stevens, Thomas, Johnson, Davis (Yiadom), Symons, Reason, Wright, Marks (McCammon).

CITY 6   BRAINTREE 2   Attendance: 2,640.

Scorers: CITY, Chambers 15; McLaughlin 28, 41; Fyfield 37; Walker (pen) 72; Moke 85   **BRAINTREE;** Marks 45; Thomas 62.

TUESDAY, October 11th took City to the seaside to visit Haig Avenue, the home of Southport, a side who were lurking just outside the play-offs, having won more games on their travels than at home. City remained unchanged for the third game in a row.

It was a game of few chances, certainly in the first half. The slippery surface didn't help matters much. McLaughlin had a 20 yard effort which went sailing wide, and Southport's Simon Grand headed wide from a corner.

Jason Walker had a chip shot deflected into keeper McMillan's hands, and then City's 11-goal marksman found himself in a spot of bother. Walker clipped Southport's Andy Owens in an off-the-ball incident, and the home fans were baying for blood. He escaped with a yellow card. Southport's James Smith was not so lucky though.

Having seemed to have tackled Chambers cleanly, the full back was astonished to be given his marching orders by referee Rob Merchant, and City had a man advantage yet again.

Kerr and Chambers missed half-chances before the break.

In the second half, City pressed ahead, with their man advantage. Chris Smith had a header saved, then Chambers had a wayward shot disappear into the night sky, and miles off target.

Not long afterwards, Chambers made amends. Scotty Kerr made a run from the halfway line, and sent him for a clear run on goal. Chambers obliged, and swung a looping, dipping shot over the keeper, as he stood transfixed on his line.

City should have closed up shop, and finished up as winners, but it wasn't to be that night. Jamal Fyfield had done brilliantly keeping out McGurk from City's line-up in the last 3 games. He was due to make his first error.

Sadly for Jamal, he made a careless pass across the edge of City's box, and Karl Ledsham intercepted. He squared it for substitute Vinny Mukendi to gleefully snap up the chance and slot in off the post. City had thrown away 2 points. This time there was no City comeback. Michael Potts did hit the post in the dying seconds but that was it.

A win would have put City 3rd, ahead of Fleetwood. As it was, they remained in 4th position as Luton were pegged back at Ebbsfleet after being 2 up with 10 minutes to go. Fleetwood surprisingly went down 4-1 at home to Newport, but City failed to capitalise on that. Wrexham and Gateshead had no game, the Welshmen having beaten the Heed at their place a week earlier.

SOUTHPORT: McMillan, James Smith, Akrigg, Grand, Owens, Whalley, Pokji, Moogan, Ledsham, Gray (Mukendi), Dan Walker (Lever 46).

YORK CITY: Ingham, Challinor, Meredith, Kerr, Smith, Fyfield, Boucaud (Potts 77), McLaughlin, Walker, Chambers, Blair.

Subs not used: Parslow, McGurk, Reed, Moke.

SOUTHPORT 1   CITY 1   Attendance: 1,107.

Scorers: SOUTHPORT, Mukendi 81   **CITY,** Chambers 62.

On October 15th, the Mariners came to Bootham, having made a mediocre start to the season, they were sitting 12th at kick off. They were backed by the largest contingent of away supporters seen this season, with 897 people from the seaside town.

Those supporters were singing at the start, and after 4 minutes the Mariners, (in all white strip with red socks), took the lead, surprisingly. A chipped cross from the right of the box found skipper Craig Disley, who beat his marker, Smith to head past Ingham.

City were undaunted, and launched a series of attacks, with quick passing and movement which was reminiscent of their early season form. Some of it was breathtaking to watch, and it was a feature of the entire game. One particular flowing move involving Meredith, Kerr, Blair, and Walker ended with the latter heading powerfully at keeper McKeown who managed to hold on to it. Wave after wave of City raids kept coming, but all to no avail.

City had been threatening for the 30 minutes or so since the Mariners had scored, but then came such a subliminal moment in the game that nobody on this Planet would have been able to believe, had they not seen it for themselves. I was one of the lucky ones to have seen it live, but it all happened so quickly that none of us who were there on the day could totally appreciate the brilliance of it all.

Firstly, Andre Boucaud swept another inch perfect, pitch-width pass to Challinor on the right. The City full-back whipped over a cross to the far post, and Scott Garner, the Grimsby centre back headed it into the air. Jason Walker was lurking in oceans of space adjacent to the penalty spot; in a flash, he waited for the ball to come down, laid back, and thumped an exquisite bicycle kick clean over two Town defenders, into the corner of the net. That was a goal worthy of being a match winner anywhere in the World, and its quality was just pure magic. It had only brought City back on level terms, but that goal was the best that I have ever witnessed at the Crescent. Talk about Rooney's bicycle kick against their City rivals last season, well this was just as good in anybody's book. I understand the goal was soon given worldwide acclaim on the Internet for weeks afterwards, and somebody told me it had received over half a million views by the end of the month. That goal had really put City on the map, and had not harmed the transfer value of Mr Walker, either.

The Grimsby fans had their hands on their heads in massive disbelief. Walker was surrounded by a pile of team-mates jumping all over him, and the Shippo fans were back in full voice once again. City still had work to do. Town almost regained their lead just before the break, but Ingham managed to avert the danger, happily.

Half-time chat was all about that wonder-goal by Mr Walker. Even the pragmatic "Fletch" had seemed to be impressed by it. "Fletch" was one of those characters who never seems to show much emotion about anything that goes on on the football park, he just takes everything in his stride, good or bad. To be fair he manages to attend most of City's away games, but is more concerned about the cost of his half-time coffee, than with matters on the pitch.

Everyone was impressed, but City still had a game to win. Grimsby were a handful, and were creating plenty more chances than City would have liked. The dangerous Liam Hearn fired narrowly wide, and substitute Anthony Elding chased on to a through ball, but drove his shot wide of Ingham's post.

City were still pressing for the winner, sporadically, and there was nothing between the sides for most of the second half. Adriano Moke had once again joined the action late on, and he enjoyed one or two lively romps along his wing.

Four minutes from time, he managed to pull the ball back for Ashley Chambers, who turned in an instant, and swept the ball into the net. City 2, Grimsby Town 1. It was a hard-earned victory by City, over a more than useful side, but the three points had sent the City faithful home happy.

No prizes for guessing where I was going after the match.

It had been a brilliant comeback by City to win the match, but all in all, their flowing football throughout had been entertaining, and victory was probably just about what City deserved. The main thing was that City were getting acclaim from the Media, in non-league circles, naturally enough, in praising their slick, passing style of play.

The added memory of that magnificent Walker goal as well, was something that would have the City fans singing for a long time to come, I can tell you.

City's third successive home win had kept them in 4th place in the table. We were now ahead of Gateshead, who had been trounced by Luton 5-1 (and that was a worrying sign as well). The Hatters were now back ahead of City on goal difference. Fleetwood, in 2nd, had won at Lincoln on Friday night, and the Wrexham bandwagon just kept rolling on. They were still top after beating Stockport 4-0 at home.

YORK CITY: Ingham, Challinor, Meredith, Kerr, Smith, Fyfield, Boucaud (Moke 77), McLaughlin, Walker (Parslow 89), Chambers, Blair.

Subs not used: Reed, McGurk, Potts.

GRIMSBY TOWN: McKeown, Silk, Kempson, Garner, Ridley, Disley, Church, Artus, Coulson, Duffy (Elding), Hearn.

CITY 2   GRIMSBY 1   Attendance: 3,872.

Scorers: CITY, Walker 34; Chambers 86   **GRIMSBY,** Disley 4.

Next up, on the following Tuesday, Cambridge United visited the Crescent. In their striking department they had one Michael Gash, who had been a favourite with many City fans. The odds against him scoring against the Minstermen were fairly high.

This was my work-mate Dave's first visit of the season. I was all set to take him in my car, but we cadged a lift with Graham and

Faye instead. Dave reckoned that he had actually met Gash's dad when he was living in the Gillingham area many years ago.

Cambridge were lurking just below City in the table, a mere point behind, and we could not afford to lose this one.

Straight away City shot themselves in the foot once again. In the 8th minute, that man Gash (who had shone in City's defeat at Wembley in the 2010 play-offs), headed on for Dunk to score easily past the startled Ingham, and we were in the mire once again.

Not for the first time, City came storming back. In the 21st minute, McLaughlin produced his trademark, mazy run at the Cambridge defence, beating three defenders, but his shot was parried by Naisbitt. Jason Walker pounced on the loose ball, and headed in his 13th goal of the season. Not as spectacular as his last one, but it would do for now.

Sadly, City let it slip again, and were behind just 10 minutes later. There were no prizes for guessing who the scorer was. Michael Gash became the 5th ex-City player this season to score against the Minstermen, as he found himself unmarked when a cross came over, and planted his header wide of a helpless Ingham. You could have bet on it.

Cambridge hardly mustered a shot in anger between their goals, and after them, but City's fighting spirit was required yet again. In the second half, it was all City. Chambers had a low shot saved, and Walker was off-target from a corner. Chambers went close from a free-kick, and then McLaughlin, and usual sub, Moke had shots saved. It was surely only a matter of time till City would be level.

Chambers tried to emulate Walker's wonder goal with an attempted overhead kick.

"There's only one Jason Walker", mocked the Shippo-ites.

And there was.

After more efforts from ex-Cambridge man, Challinor, and Moke had missed the target, the latter won a free-kick with one of his dazzling "romps" along the left. He was brought down in full flow just outside the box.

It was time for Mr Walker to take centre stage. City's now World famous striker stepped up, and whipped a curling shot beyond the despairing keeper to his right. Cue, delirium in the Shippo. We all had a group hug in celebration. It was no more than City deserved, and it was Walker's 14th of the season.

A win would have been no more than City deserved, but it failed to come. Even that man Walker is human after all. He managed to miss what for him was an easy chance by blasting over the roof of the Shippo from 15 yards after yet another City free-kick.

No matter, we had still denied Cambridge from overtaking us in the league standings. That was something to be grateful for.

City actually moved up to 3rd place with their point, as Luton had been scalped by Wrexham at Kenilworth Road. The Dragons were flying now, 4 points ahead of Fleetwood who won 4-1 at Alfreton. Southport had sneaked into 4th spot ahead of Luton, with their win at Gateshead, who themselves were falling fast. Cambridge were 6th.

YORK CITY: Ingham, Challinor, Meredith, Kerr, Smith, Fyfield, Boucaud (Potts 74), McLaughlin (Reed 74), Walker, Chambers, Blair (Moke 54).

Subs not used: Parslow, McGurk.

CAMBRIDGE UNITED: Naisbitt, Thorpe (Wilde), Coulson, McAuley, Jennings, Carew, Jarvis, Shaw, Dunk, (Winn), Berry (Charles), Gash.

CITY 2   CAMBRIDGE 2   **Attendance:** 2,711.

Scorers: **CITY,** Walker 21, 89   **CAMBRIDGE,** Dunk 8; Gash 31.

Hayes and Yeading were struggling just outside the bottom 4 in the Conference. Free-scoring City must have been the last team they would want to face at this stage of the season. Another ex-City striker, Richard Pacquette was in their starting line-up.

As expected, the Minstermen were the superior force throughout the first half. Apart from an off-target header from Pacquette, it was City who had the majority of possession, and chances were coming thick and fast.

James Meredith was unceremoniously hacked down on 14 minutes, and it was Walker's chance again. He curled yet another one straight into the keeper's top right hand corner to claim his 15th of the season.

Just 4 minutes later one of City's slick passing moves saw Scotty Kerr sending Challinor down the right. The full-back twisted and turned, before firing in from an angle for his first goal in City colours, and the Minstermen were well in command.

Then, the unthinkable of unthinkables happened. Walker limped off with what was later described as a "sore achilles" on 37 minutes. The City faithful hoped and prayed it wasn't a serious injury that would keep our top scorer out of the action for too long. Obviously he was vital to City's hopes of staying in the play-off spots, with his 15 goals in 18 games so far.

Typically, City lost their concentration once again, in the last minute of the first half, allowing Soares to run on to the ball, and glance a header past the startled Ingham.

Moke was once again enjoying his role as substitute, and he was terrorizing the Hayes defenders. He ghosted past their giddy full-back numerous times, as City blazed on for another strike. It wasn't long before it came. Moke started the move with a pass to Chambers, who fed the ball to Paddy McLaughlin who cracked in a shot from 25 yards which flew past keeper Arnold's lug-hole into the corner of the net.

It was all City once again. Boucaud had a go at impersonating Moke with his tricky footwork, but he was never likely to add to his single goal in goodness-knows how many appearances. His shot went sailing wide.

Moke again burst past full-back Fraser Franks, who must have been as dizzy as a drunken sop by now. The ball was crossed from the by-line into the path of Chambers, who paused before smartly, side-footing in City's 4th from the edge of the six-yard box, and it was time to start the car.

Or not quite, yet. Once again City's defence slacked off in the last minute, when Williams was allowed the time and space to drive a bus through City's back four, he took the opportunity to force the ball past Ingham, for a flattering 4-2 scoreline in City's favour. Nobody was complaining too much after City's 4th win out of the last 6 games. It only remained to see just how serious Walker's injury was.

City remained handily placed in 3rd, a point ahead of Luton who had won at Grimsby (not an easy task) .Wrexham's march was somewhat halted by their fellow countrymen from Newport who claimed a 0-0 draw at the Racecourse. Fleetwood beat Bath 4-1 at home.

HAYES AND YEADING: Arnold, Franks, (Argent), Cadmore, Ujah, John, Crockford (Lee), Mackie (Collins), Bentley, Williams, Pacquette, Soares.

YORK CITY: Ingham, Challinor, Meredith, Kerr, Smith, Fyfield, Boucaud, McLaughlin, (Potts 88),Walker (Moke 37), Chambers (Reed 79), Blair.

Subs not used: McGurk, Parslow.

HAYES 2   CITY 4   Attendance: 525.

Scorers: HAYES, Soares 45; Williams 90   **CITY,** Walker 14; Challinor 19; McLaughlin 62; Chambers 76.

Now it was FA Cup time once again. The 4th Qualifying Round, on October 29th. There was no harder possible task for City, who had to face the top non-league side, Wrexham, at their place.

Walker was obviously out of the side. Nobody knew whether his injury was serious or not. Gary Mills had decided to 'rest' no less than 6 of his men, who had all played in the same line up for the last 6 games, as well. Challinor, Smith, Fyfield, Boucaud, Chambers, and Blair all missed out, in favour of Oyebanjo, McGurk, Parslow, Potts, Henderson, and Reed.

If nothing else, it seemed like City's squad had quality in depth. It remained to be seen whether they could carry on where the "first" team left off.

They could not.

Wrexham wanted revenge for their 3-0 drubbing by City at the Racecourse in September, and they got it.

City's new side looked toothless, without Walker, Chambers and Blair. They were a shadow of their former selves it seemed.

The Dragons had a fairly young side themselves. Chances were few and far between in the first half. Wrexham had a penalty shout when Jake Speight appeared to have been pushed in the box, but referee Jeremy Simpson wasn't having any of it. Knight-Percival headed wide, and then McGurk appeared to use his hand, but again the referee declined to point to the spot.

Wrexham had the better of things but the score remained goalless at the interval.

But not for long. The out-of-sorts Moke gave away a needless free-kick in the 50th minute, and City were punished for it. Knight-Percival headed Wrexham into the lead.

Eight minutes later, though, City were awarded a free-kick of their own. Paddy McLaughlin stepped up, and in a perfect impersonation of Jason Walker, he curled the ball in around Wrexham's young keeper, and City were, somewhat fortunately, still in the tie.

Liam Henderson had taken up Walker's central striker role, and had a decent effort deflected wide, and then drove high and wide from 30 yards a few moments later. City were doing fine, to hold on, but they were far from the team which had destroyed the Welshmen 6 weeks earlier.

Wrexham manager Andy Morrell brought himself on, with almost immediate success. The veteran striker retrieved a long pass to the far post, and drove the ball across the 6-yard line for the unfortunate McGurk to slice his attempted clearance past the helpless Ingham, and City were dumped out of the Cup.

Never mind. We could now concentrate on the League. It was mid-season now. Let's see what the month of November will bring.

WREXHAM: Mayebi, Obeng, Creighton, Knight-Percival, Ashton, Harris (Fowler), Clarke, Hunt, Cieslewicz, Pogba (Morrell), Speight (Wright).

YORK CITY: Ingham, Oyebanjo, Meredith, Kerr, McGurk, Parslow, Potts (Challinor 77) McLaughlin, Henderson, Reed (Blair 68), Moke (Chambers 68). **Subs not used:** Musselwhite, Smith, Boucaud, Fyfield.

WREXHAM 2   CITY 1   Attendance: 2,252.

Scorers: WREXHAM, Knight-Percival 50; McGurk (og) 81
       CITY, McLaughin 58.

BLUE SQUARE NATIONAL CONFERENCE
AT 28 OCTOBER 2011 (TOP 12)

1.	Wrexham..	18	12	3	3	33-14	39
2.	Fleetwood	18	11	4	3	37-24	37
3.	YORK CITY	18	10	4	4	39-21	34
4.	Luton Town	18	9	6	3	34-18	33
5.	Cambridge	18	9	6	3	27-16	33
6.	Gateshead	18	10	3	5	31-28	33
7.	Southport	18	9	5	4	29-27	32
8.	Mansfield T	17	8	6	3	29-21	30
9.	Braintree T	18	9	2	7	37-29	29
10.	Tamworth	17	8	5	4	23-17	29
11.	Barrow	18	9	2	7	32-30	29
12.	Kidderminster	18	8	4	6	32-29	28

CHAPTER 6

NOVEMBER: HANGING ON IN THERE

THE first Saturday in November saw the Dragons coming back to Bootham Crescent, fresh from their FA Cup success over City seven days earlier. This was Bonfire Night and there may have been a few fireworks expected.

Jason Walker returned, his injury not being as serious as was initially thought, together with Smith and Fyfield in central defence, Ashley Chambers, and Matty Blair. City were eager to do the double over the green-clad Dragons.

Table-toppers Wrexham looked dangerous when they broke from deep. A cross from Cieslewiez was met by Jamie Tolley who produced a bullet header which Ingham managed to save, having changed direction in an instant.

Ingham was forced to make another eye-catching save from player manager Morrell at point blank range. It was a stirring tussle in the main, despite the lack of any goals. McLaughlin just cleared the angle with a rasping drive as both sides went at it, Hammer and Tongs.

Chambers had a 70 yard diagonal run which finished up with his shot, off balance, being saved by Mayebi.

Much the same in the second half. Two accomplished passing sides cancelled each other out, and no side had the upper hand really. Moke burst down the right, and cut inside, but his angled shot was comfortably saved.

Another sweeping move involving new skipper Kerr, Boucaud, and Walker ended up with Challinor having a 20 yarder saved again.

A point would do for City, grudgingly, though three would have been tremendous. Ingham made the save of the match, diving full length to save another Morrell header.

Moke, on the right this time was not as dangerous as his former self, but managed another similar effort cutting inside his marker, and had his shot saved once again.

Wrexham almost clinched it late, late on. A dangerous cross caught Smithy napping, and Ingham pushed the ball off Danny Wright's toes to force a corner. Nothing came of it, and the points were shared.

All in all, City were still effective going forward, yet still resolute at the back against the leaders of the Division. Scotty Kerr was instrumental as an extra defender, if you like, and his work-rate in cutting out dangerous through balls was admirable.

Four points out of six, and no goals conceded was a good return against the leaders, although City slipped to 4th as Cambridge won at Mansfield. In the other big match of the day, Fleetwood won at Luton, and were level on points with Wrexham, with an inferior goal difference of five. Luton were down to 7th place.

YORK CITY: Ingham, Challinor, Meredith, Kerr, Smith, Fyfield, Boucaud (Potts 84), McLaughlin, Walker, Chambers, Blair (Moke 35).

Subs not used: McGurk, Parslow, Reed.

CITY 0   WREXHAM 0   Attendance: 4,295.

WREXHAM: Mayebi, Obeng, Creighton, Knight-Percival, Ashton, Clarke, Tolley (Fowler), Harris, Morrell (Wright), Pogba, Cieslewiez (Hunt).

At Barrow on the following Tuesday it was a case of two strikers facing up against their former clubs. Jason Walker had been a favourite at Holker Street, and Barrow's Adam Boyes had played a minor role in City's play-off charge in 2010.

City seemed lacklustre in the main, and Barrow had the better of the first half. Adam Boyes had netted 12 times this season (including one against City, of course), and had a couple of chances early on. Michael Ingham again produced a stunning save to keep the Cumbrians off the scoresheet. Richie Baker curled a free-kick over City's wall and the City keeper had to be at his brilliant best to keep it out.

Once again, midfield General Scotty Kerr was doing a magnificent impression of Tottenham's Scott Parker, hassling and harrying everything that moved, and making sure the danger from Barrow's midfield raiders was averted.

City looked a little brighter on the resumption. A Chambers cross for Walker was saved by Danny Hurst as the City marksman hunted for his 16th of the season. Andy Cook forced Ingham into yet another fine save with his 25 yard effort.

A shot from Chambers seemed to have struck the hand of Barrow defender Paul Smith but nothing was given. Another curling free-kick from Walker was tipped away by Hurst, and City were searching for a winner. Challinor had a run across the box, and played in Chambers who chipped his shot over the bar. It looked like being a stalemate, and so it was.

Unfortunately it wasn't quite all over. Jason Walker, deep in stoppage time, slid in on Jason Owen and the tackle hadn't really impressed referee Carl Evans. The City Talisman received his marching orders, and Andre Boucaud was also shown red in his (apparent) involvement in the boxing match that followed. Luckily City were only down to nine men for seconds, as the final whistle blew.

Two clean sheets in a row, but City needed wins not draws. At least our Jason could have a little rest. Goodness knows, we would miss him quite a lot.

Wrexham won 2-0, and stayed on top. Fleetwood won 2-1, and Cambridge drew 1-1 with Luton. City stayed in 5th, but just a mere point ahead of Gateshead.

BARROW: Hurst, Bolland, Hone, Skelton, Rutherford, Baker, Owen, Smith, Mackreth, (Rowe), Cook (Almond), Boyes.

YORK CITY: Ingham, Challinor, Meredith, Kerr, Smith (McGurk 65), Fyfield, Boucaud, McLaughlin (Pilkington 59), Walker, Chambers (Parslow 90), Blair.

Subs not used: Reed, Moke.

BARROW 0   CITY 0   Attendance: 2,190.

Next up a trip to Forest Green to visit the New Lawn, in the small Gloucestershire town of Nailsworth. Forest Green were having a more than respectable season, and were lying 13th in the table. Their defensive record in only conceding 20 goals was only bettered by Wrexham and Cambridge. This would be a tough encounter.

Jon Challinor reverted to midfield for City, and Oyebanjo was recalled at right back. City were missing the suspended Boucaud and Walker, so brand new striker Moses Ashikodi was brought into the side following his move from struggling Kettering.

Nothing happened in the first half of very special interest. City threatened on numerous occasions but nothing came of their efforts. The home side were not much better. Defences were on top throughout.

The second period was not much better, from all accounts, but the home side had the first attacking move. James Rowe had a decent effort saved by Ingham in the opening seconds of the half. Forest Green's Al Bangura then shot wide from 15 yards, and Klukowski, the dangerous midfielder headed wide from a Norwood cross.

City were struggling to find their passing game. Fair to say, there hadn't been a shot in anger from the Minstermen all afternoon, as far as I can remember, as I listened to the radio coverage.

Suddenly, on 82 minutes, the game surged into life. Reedy, at long last, burst into the area, only to have his balance toppled as Jamie Turley clattered into the back of him as he prepared to shoot. The ball broke to Danny Pilkington who netted, but the whistle had already blown for a penalty.

Reedy took the kick himself, and confidently blasted it into the roof of the net to give City a very fortunate lead with only 8 minutes remaining.

In a game of so few clear chances, City would have backed themselves to win the points. Sadly, it was not to be.

Deep into stoppage time, according to Mr Parker it was the 5th minute of 4 minutes announced, Smith failed to stop a long ball downfield getting past him and bouncing out of play. From the resulting throw, Matt Taylor lashed in a teasing cross which Ingham failed to deal with, and he pushed the ball straight to substitute James Norwood who gobbled up the chance to score from 6 yards, out. It was the last kick of the match, and City had thrown away 2 points again.

I was in bits, and kicked the radio in disgust. The cat didn't fare too well either, and went scuttling out of the room having copped a bit of the rage as well. Poor cat.

Poor City as well. Goodness knows how costly those lost 2 points would be, come April 28th (ironically our last game would be against Forest Green again). Too many draws and not enough wins. City were off the pace again.

We were still in 5th, but only headed Luton on goal-difference now. Wrexham drew at Braintree, and Fleetwood drew at Gateshead. The Hatters won at Newport County. City were 7 points off the top, and, in my belief, any chance of winning the title had vanished at Forest Green.

FOREST GREEN: Bond, Hodgkiss, Turley, Oshodi, Stokes, Rowe (Uwezu), Al Bangura, Forbes, Klukowski, Taylor, Griffin (Norwood).

YORK CITY: Ingham, Oyebanjo, Meredith, Kerr, Smith, Fyfield, Challinor (Parslow 89), McLaughlin (Pilkington 79); Ashikodi (Reed 73), Chambers, Blair.

Subs not used: McGurk, Moke.

FOREST GREEN 1   CITY 1   Attendance: 1,157.

Scorers: FOREST GREEN, Norwood 90+5   **CITY,** Reed (pen) 83.

LINCOLN CITY had come down from the Football League, along with Stockport. They were struggling just above the relegation places, and needed the points urgently, but so did City.

Smithy was dropped to the bench as McGurk was recalled, and Jamie Reed made the starting line-up as did Danny Pilkington, his second start in a City shirt. Boucaud and Walker were still suspended. The Imps had former City winger Simon Russell in their side.

Straight from the start, Conal Platt gave City a scare, but drove over the bar from close range, as if it was a wake-up call for City if they needed one.

If it was, it surely worked. Three minutes later Pilkington received the ball from his right, and 20 yards out, beat the visiting keeper with the aid of a deflection. It was just the fillip City needed to get back on track again.

James Meredith fired across from an angle, and then Russell shot wide at the other end in an attempt to become the 6th City "exile" to score against the Minstermen this season. Reedy and Matty Blair both had headers which failed to find the net, and City held on comfortably to their advantage. It was unusual to see us attacking the visitors end in the second spell, I believe that was the first occasion it had happened this season. Ashley Chambers missed a glorious chance from 5 yards out as he scuffed his shot, disappointingly wide.

Matty Blair was running through the Imps midfield at will, he released the ball to McLaughlin who curled the ball into Farman's bottom corner to give City a more comfortable lead.

This time City coasted comfortably to the final whistle without any horrible lapses which had been occurring far too often in recent games. Another win, and their undefeated run had extended to 10 games in the League, albeit having drawn no less than 5 of those.

That Tuesday night, Fleetwood won 3-0 at home to hapless Kettering, who were suffering horrendous financial woes, and were next to visit City. Luton drew at home to Telford. Wrexham had no game but defeated Darlington at home on the following evening. City stayed in 4th, now 2 points clear of 6th place Luton. A bit of breathing space had developed, but not much.

YORK CITY: Ingham, Challinor, Meredith, Kerr, McGurk, Fyfield, Pilkington (Ashikodi 76), McLaughlin, Reed, Chambers (Oyebanjo 87), Blair.

Subs not used: Smith, Parslow, Moke.

LINCOLN CITY: Farman, Sinclair, Hinds, Gowling, Nutter, Russell (Laurent), Power, Thompson, Platt, Sheridan (Nicolau), Perry (Medley).

CITY 2   LINCOLN 0   **Attendance:** 3,155.

Scorers: CITY, Pilkington 4; McLaughlin 58.

BLUE SQUARE CONFERENCE TABLE
AT 29 NOVEMBER 2011 (TOP 12)

1.	Fleetwood	22	14	5	3	45-27	47
2.	Wrexham	21	13	5	3	35-14	44
3.	Southport	22	12	5	5	36-33	41
4.	YORK CITY	22	11	7	4	42-22	40
5.	Cambridge	22	10	9	3	31-19	39
6.	Luton Town	22	10	8	4	38-22	38
7.	Gateshead	22	10	7	5	36-33	37
8.	Kidderminster	22	10	6	6	40-33	36
9.	Forest Green	22	8	9	5	35-22	33
10.	Mansfield T	21	8	9	4	32-25	33
11.	Tamworth	21	9	6	6	26-23	33
12.	Barrow	22	10	3	9	34-33	33

CHAPTER 7

DECEMBER: THE FA TROPHY TRAIL BEGINS

DECEMBER was here, and City were handily placed in 4th position, unbeaten in 10 League games, and hoping to extend that run further against Kettering Town, who were in dire financial straights, and were in danger of folding. City had already acquired 2 of their former players this season, in Jon Challinor and Moses Ashikodi, both of whom figured in the 5-1 demolition by City at their place in the first month of the season.

Challinor was in City's starting line up, and Ashikodi was on the bench. Jason Walker and Andre Boucaud were both missing their 3rd game due to suspension.

Kettering's plight was such that they could only name two substitutes for the game.

Buoyed up from their success in August, City went for Kettering's jugular from the off. In the 6th minute, Reedy got the ball rolling as he found himself in enough space to swing a cat, and gobbled up an easy chance to head past hapless Aldi Haxhia to put City 1-0 up.

Next, Reedy headed over from a Chambers cross, and in truth, he should have had a hat-trick inside 12 minutes. He did manage his second, with another header, after Pilkington fed new skipper Kerr, who provided the perfect cross to head in his second out of three attempts, in spite of Sol Davis unsuccessful attempt to clear off the line.

This was followed by a sweeping move involving Fyfield, Meredith, Blair and Chambers, which ended up with McLaughlin hitting the post from an acute angle. The rebound went straight to Jon Challinor who calmly side-footed into the net from 10 yards out to put City 3 up, and in total control.

Kettering did manage a shot in anger on 40 minutes from Josh Dawkins but his effort cleared the roof of the Longhurst stand. Even then they had another attempt as David Bridges shot weakly, straight at Michael Ingham.

In first half stoppage time, City made it four. Kerr sent Chambers down the left, pulled the ball back, and Matty Blair drilled it in past hapless Haxhia. City 4, Kettering 0 at the interval.

There was to be no let-off from the Minstermen. Blair passed to McLaughlin on 50 minutes, and the young Irishman tore into the box, beat a challenge or two, and blasted it through the hands of the young Albanian keeper. You had to feel sorry for Kettering now. At least I did.

Ashikodi had now replaced Reedy, at half-time, to torment his former team-mates. He collected a long clearance from Ingham, and crossed to Pilkington, who squared it to Chambers who fired in past Haxhia to make it six. There were still 25 minutes to go.

Some 12 minutes later, Ashikodi, having missed an earlier chance did manage to score against his former club after McLaughlin provided the chance from the goal line, and the grateful newcomer to City's ranks blasted in from an acute angle. In celebration he took off his shirt, and waved it in glee to the Shippo-ites.

In the 92nd minute City could, and should have equalled their record 8-goal winning margin, but to his eternal credit, the heroic Kettering keeper pulled off a blinding save from Ashikodi's downward header. It was no more than the young man deserved to know that he had denied City that proud record. 7-0 it stayed. Ashikodi consoled the young keeper at the final whistle.

So this was another "Fish and Chips" moment I suppose. We only hoped and prayed that this result, and the 5-1 away win against the Poppies would not be expunged from the record books should Kettering go under. City were clear in 4th by now. Wrexham, Fleetwood and Luton were all involved in the FA Cup second round. Wrexham actually won at Brentford. Fleetwood drew with Yeovil on Friday night, and Luton went down 4-2 to Cheltenham.

YORK CITY: Ingham, Challinor, Meredith, Kerr (Oyebanjo 58), McGurk, Fyfield, Pilkington, McLaughlin, Reed (Ashikodi 46), Chambers (Moke 68), Blair.

Subs not used: Smith, Parslow.

KETTERING: Haxhia, Noubissie, Ifil, Swaibu, Davis, Navarro, Bridges, O'Leary, (Pryor 23), Deeney, Dawkin, Hughes-Mason.

Sub not used: Dance.

CITY 7   KETTERING 0   Attendance: 2,899.

Scorers: CITY, Reed 6, 12; Challinor 30; Blair 45 + 3; McLaughlin 50, Chambers 65; Ashikodi 77.

Ashley Chambers scores the 6th goal as the Minstermen go goal crazy.
(Picture The Press, York).

On the following Tuesday since their ebullient display against the hapless Poppies, City went to the New Bucks Head, the home of Telford, intent on revenge for their earlier home defeat, and intent on extending their 11-run unbeaten sequence.

It was a game of attrition throughout. Cat and mouse, if you like to call it that. Most of the action was happening in the middle of the park, and both sides were sparring like a couple of cagey boxers but nobody could land the sucker punch.

Everything City threw at Telford they repelled. Telford put men behind the ball and broke sporadically into City's half. Ashley Chambers shot wide, and Paddy McLaughlin sent a header wide as well.

Fyfield tidied up after Ingham mishandled, and then the City keeper redeemed himself to stop a cross-cum-shot from Valentine from beating him. Scotty Kerr missed a chance from close in, but to be fair, he had to stretch for it. He had yet to score in 22 games for City.

Just before the break, Telford's Nathan Rooney had the best chance of the half, finding himself unmarked, he wasted the chance, and headed over the bar.

In the second half, Telford did come out of their shell. McGurk headed off the line from David Preston, and Ingham saved well from a powerful shot by Trainer. Brown shot wide from the edge of the box.

City were now under pressure, and battling to save a precious point. Ashley Cain poked his shot wide as Ingham rushed out to block, and then the same player shot straight at Ingham from close range.

Substitute Danny Pilkington was providing City's best option, as the returning Jason Walker seemed far below his normal fitness levels. McLaughlin came close on 83 minutes, but not close enough.

There was just time for Cain and Preston to threaten City one more time, but the Minstermen hung on grimly. Super-sub Reedy came on for Boucaud, and almost snatched an undeserved winner, as he turned and shot over the bar. Grudgingly, a point would have to be enough. Again.

City moved to 3rd, as Southport lost at Wrexham. Luton drew at Lincoln. Fleetwood had no game.

AFC TELFORD: Young, Salmon, Whitehead, Preston, Valentine, Cain, Trainer, Smith, Newton, Jones (Rooney), Brown.

YORK CITY: Ingham, Challinor, Meredith, Kerr, Smith, Fyfield, Boucaud (Reed 70) McLaughlin, Walker (Ashikodi 79), Chambers (Pilkington 46), Blair.

TELFORD 0   CITY 0   Attendance: 1,601.

Subs not used: Oyebanjo, Smith.

On December the 10th, it was FA Trophy time again. Last season City lost at home to Boston United at the first hurdle, now it was the turn of Solihull Moors from the Conference North, to try and make a name for themselves.

They certainly did just that. The West Midlanders came out of the traps from minute one, and caught lethargic City on the hop. A cross from Lee Morris found Jordan Fitzpatrick, who gleefully put away the visitors first chance inside 3 minutes.

City's response was clinical. After a McLaughlin free-kick was saved by Singh, a cross by Danny Pilkington was headed in by Matty Blair at the far post to make it 1-1 with only 6 minutes gone.

Pilkington really should have scored midway through the half, but shot wide as the onrushing keeper pressured him. Solihull striker Richard Walker missed from close range, and fired over Ingham's bar.

The same striker made amends a few minutes later by beating the offside trap, and Dave McGurk, and planting a smart shot on the turn, past Michael Ingham. 2-1 to the Moors at half-time.

There was a lack of urgency in the second half as well. Even when they pressed, the Moors men hassled, and harried constantly, and, according to our Mr Parker, they seemed to be taking their time to take their throw-ins and set pieces. Fair play to them, their game plan was to stop City getting into their stride, and it worked, in the main.

City had a massive penalty claim when Stuart Pierpoint clearly handled a Matty Blair shot on the goal line, but the officials hadn't seen the incident.

City were on their way out of the trophy at the first attempt, deep into stoppage time. In a last gasp effort, Moke launched the ball into the box. Jon Challinor slid into the keeper, and the ball ran loose. Instead of blowing up for a foul on the keeper, play went on and Challinor put the ball into the empty net. The goal was given.

Solihull's supporters must have been enraged at such injustice. Their players had worked their socks off, and they probably deserved their victory.

City were decidedly lucky to live to fight another day. How important that injury time decision might turn out to be, well, only time would tell.

YORK CITY: Ingham, Challinor, Meredith, (Parslow 80), Kerr, McGurk, Fyfield, Boucaud (Ashikodi 39), McLaughlin, Walker, Pilkington (Moke 6), Blair.

Subs not used: Smith, Potts.

SOLIHULL MOORS: Singh, Midworth, Spencer, Pierpoint, Langdon, (Melligan), (Francis 86), Fitzpatrick, Hurren, English, Blackwood, Morris, R Walker (Johnson).

CITY 2   SOLIHULL 2   Attendance: 1,116.

Scorers: CITY, Blair 6; Challinor 90+3   **SOLIHULL,** Fitzpatrick 3; R Walker 40.

Grateful still to be in the Trophy, City faced a first ever visit to Damson Park, on a cold December Tuesday for the replay. These are the places where your dreams of winning the Trophy do begin. These games have to be won, if you want that success.

City set about their task like the polished, professionals that they were, and put the Moors under pressure from the start. On 11 minutes, Chris Smith made a run towards the far post. Scott Kerr's cross picked him up perfectly, Smithy nodded in, and City were on their way.

Apparently, the radio chaps had problems installing their equipment at the ground, but managed to keep us in the picture, in the main. Apparently Solihull had a few chances, but there was no more scoring in the first half.

Just after the hour mark, Paddy McLaughlin made a raking pass in the general direction of Matty Blair on the opposite flank. The nippy winger raced on to it like a greyhound, and went on to prod the ball into the net, as keeper Singh came dashing out.

City were home and hosed soon after that. A cross from Meredith was cleared, but it came to Matty Blair who volleyed in from 15 yards, for his second of the game, and 6th of the season.

City were on the march. They had been given a lucky break in the first game, but never looked back. Who knows how much they would live to be thankful for their first game reprieve.

SOLIHULL MOORS: Singh, Karonji, Pierpoint (Broadhurst), Spencer, Francis, Fitzpatrick, Hurren, Blackwood, Johnson, Morris (Jackson), R Walker (Beswick)

YORK CITY: Ingham, Parslow, Challinor, Smith, McGurk, Fyfield, Kerr, McLaughlin, (Pilkington 87), J Walker, Blair (Moke 82), Meredith.

Subs not used: Ashikodi, Potts, Boucaud.

SOLIHULL 0   CITY 3   Attendance: 275.

Scorers: CITY, Smith 11; Blair 62, 77.

CITY had no game on Saturday December 17th, as they were playing on Monday night. It was a horrible day for City fans as

Wrexham, Fleetwood, Luton, and Southport all won. City were still 4th, but were now a massive 9 points off the leaders.

Premier Sports TV were here. City had never fared too well with the cameras present, as history will tell you. The pessimists among the City ranks (and some say I am one of those), never gave us much hope of winning on that night. Kidderminster are one of City's bogey teams as well.

Andre Boucaud and Ashley Chambers returned for City. Jason Walker was missing, sadly, as his injury had been aggravated in the last couple of games. Matty Blair was facing his former mates.

City gave Kidderminster an early Christmas present, and a flying start to the game. The Harriers were quicker out of their blocks, and after they had had a corner in the 2nd minute, resulting in a shot going wide, they kept the pressure up. In the 5th minute Mickey Demetriou launched a free-kick into the box, and unmarked Jack Byrne headed in.

Kidderminster kept up their high tempo passing game, and Matt forced Ingham into a save, and Gittings latched on to a mistake by McLaughlin but his shot was deflected over. City were well and truly under the cosh. It was clear that the Harriers were liking the cameras far more than City were.

However, City's first attack on 20 minutes did prove fruitful. At last, Chambers broke free down the right, and crossed for Matty Blair to tap in from close range. A bit unfair on Kidderminster, but City were not complaining.

What goes around comes around. Kidderminster were not messing about, and back they came like a yellow tornado. Within a minute of City's leveller, they were back in front. Callum Gittings shrugged off a tackle by Jon Challinor, and fired the Harriers into the lead, off Ingham's post.

Worse was to follow. City were all but buried by half-time. The Harriers extended their lead further on 33 minutes. Poor Jamal Fyfield who had performed well of late, had lost the ball to Jamille

Matt, who galloped away, before Fyfield caught him up, then missed his tackle again, and Matt fired in from 10 yards to make it 3-1.

City were scuppered. Yes, they had plenty of spirit, but they had a mountain to climb in the second half. It would certainly make for good TV if we could do it. The pessimists among our ranks were far from hopeful. Not me, honestly.

Gary Mills changed things soon after the break. He brought on Moke and Ashikodi in place of Boucaud and Pilkington, with Ashikodi joining Chambers in a 4-4-2 set up.

On 63 minutes City were back in with a shout. The ball hit the arm of Luke Jones as Chambers tried to get past him. With Jason Walker missing, Chambers took the kick himself. His weak effort was easily pushed away by Breeden, and it was back to square one.

Far from being deflated, City's spirit shone again. They won a corner on the right, and McGurk headed in for his first off the season as he got there just before Tom Sharpe. Hope was still springing eternal, just.

All City's efforts came to nought. Matty Blair shot straight at Breeden. Parslow was brought on as an extra striker (believe it or believe it not). At the death, even Michael Ingham ventured up front but it was Kidderminster who would have a Happy Christmas, and not the Minstermen. City remained 4th.

YORK CITY: Ingham, Challinor, Meredith, Kerr, McGurk, Fyfield, Boucaud (Moke 53), McLaughlin, Pilkington (Ashikodi 53), Chambers (Parslow 84), Blair.

Subs not used: Oyebanjo, Smith.

KIDDERMINSTER: Breeden, Vaughan, Jones, Demetriou, Sharpe, Byrne, Storer, Hendrie (Marc Williams), Hankin, Matt (Guinan), Gittings (Wright).

CITY 2   KIDDERMINSTER 3   Attendance: 2,830.

Scorers: CITY, Blair 20; McGurk 67   **KIDDERMINSTER,** Byrne 5; Gittings 21; Matt 33.

A trip to Field Mill on Boxing Day would be no joy-ride for City either. Mansfield were lurking just below the play-offs but they had a game in hand on City. A win for the Stags would have brought them seriously into contention for the top 5 places.

Matt Green had broken City's hearts in the 2010 play-off Final for his part in helping Oxford to shatter City's dreams. He had already scored 14 times for the Stags this season. For City, Oyebanjo came in at right-back at the expense of Challinor, and Chris Smith came in to the back four as Fyfield was moved across to the left, to allow Meredith to join Smith and McGurk in a 3-5-2 set up.

Matthew Green rapidly reminded City what a lethal striker he is, as he gobbled up a rarely-seen careless back-pass from McGurk, and went on to round Michael Ingham with ease.

Mansfield were in control, and City hardly got a sniff of their goal, apart from the occasional counter attack. On one such occasion Matty Blair disappointingly fired straight at Marriott, and City went into the break a goal behind.

It was all Mansfield early in the second half. Dyer missed two chances, one from close in after Green made a dangerous run. The dangerous Lindon Meikle was also causing havoc running at the City defenders, on one occasion Ingham managed to save a shot by Dyer with his feet.

Matt Green was taken off on 54 minutes, and it seemed to give City a lift in confidence. Liam Henderson, enjoying his first League start somehow managed to a curl a shot from 15 yards past Marriott after a shot by Oyebanjo had landed at his feet.

Henderson, who had just returned from Forest Green on loan, made way for supersub Reedy, but for a deflection the City number 7 almost snatched an undeserved winner, but the deflection took it over the bar.

Towards the end City were in full flow, and searching for a late winner. Chambers rushed a fairly good chance, and missed the target, while Smithy headed a last gasp chance wide in the 94th minute. All in all a draw was probably a fair result on the balance of play. This was City's fourth away draw on the trot, and they were hanging in there, just.

Kidderminster, after their victory at the Crescent a week earlier, added to City's worries as they beat Forest Green, and were now lurking in 6th, on the same points as City, and Luton who were 5th after thrashing Kettering 5-0. There was no surprise in that result.

Wrexham won at Telford and stayed top. Fleetwood drew 2-2 with Southport in their top 3 local Derby at Highbury.

The year of 2011 had ended with City in 4th place, and hanging on to a play-off place by the skin of their teeth.

Gary Mills and his boys had so far done a fantastic job to get City into that position, and it was down to them to try and stay there. At the turn of the year, Jason Walker was still missing through injury (now he had a groin strain apparently). The thing was, the youngsters Gary Mills had brought in, like Walker, had bolstered City's attack, considerably.

The blistering pace of Matty Blair, and the midfield runs and long-range passing of McLaughlin had been a joy to watch. Scott Kerr had been a hard-working defensive midfielder, and he never stopped running in the engine-room of the team. Andre Boucaud's passing ability completed the brilliant City midfield. All in all, the future looked bright for 2012, and promotion was definitely on the cards. It was hoped that Gary Mills would dip into the transfer market to bolster City's squad even further for the months ahead.

MANSFIELD TOWN: Marriott, O'Neill, Riley, Dempster, Freeman, Verma, Murray, Howell, Meikle, Dyer, Green (Briscoe).

YORK CITY: Ingham, Oyebanjo, Meredith, Kerr, McGurk, Smith, Fyfield (Chambers 46), McLaughlin, Henderson (Reed 75), Parslow, Blair.

Subs not used: Potts, Boucaud, Challinor.

MANSFIELD 1   CITY 1   Attendance: 3,551.

Scorers: MANSFIELD, Green 11   **CITY,** Henderson 63.

BLUE SQUARE CONFERENCE TABLE
AT 31 DECEMBER 2011 (TOP 10)

1.	Wrexham	25	17	5	3	43-16	56
2.	Fleetwood T	25	16	6	3	51-30	54
3.	Southport	26	14	6	6	43-39	48
4.	YORK CITY	26	12	9	5	52-26	45
5.	Luton Town	25	12	9	4	47-24	45
6.	Kidderminster	25	13	6	6	48-36	45
7.	Cambridge	25	11	10	4	33-21	43
8.	Gateshead	25	11	8	6	39-36	41
9.	Mansfield T	25	9	11	5	38-30	38
10.	Barrow	25	11	5	9	37-35	38

CHAPTER 8
JANUARY 2012: NEW YEAR, NEW HOPE

SO here was 2012 at last. Another year had arrived and it could be a glorious year for all City supporters if things went our way in the last 20 games. York City won promotion to the (then) Division 2, in 1974. Then, in 1993 they won promotion to Division 2 (in its new format), after a 19 year gap. That was 19 years ago, the last time we went up. I wonder. Do things happen in sequences ???

MANSFIELD TOWN came up to Bootham, in the reverse fixture to the Boxing Day match-up. They had drawn no less than 11 of their 25 games to date, including the one against City at their place 6 days ago.

There was one New Year's resolution City had broken straight away in the first game of 2012. Their annoying habit of sleeping in the first 15 minutes had not altered. Mansfield left back Kieron Freeman raced on to a pass by Meikle, and his low cross was turned into the City net by that nemesis Matt Green to score his 3rd goal against the Minstermen in as many games. It was backs-to the-wall time for City once again.

Liam Henderson, still in Walker's role, had a decent shot saved by Marriott, and then James Meredith popped up in the Mansfield box, but placed his shot wide with only the keeper to beat. David McGurk limped off after half an hour, and Fyfield regained his place in the back four. It would be quite significant later.

Following a free-kick from Scott Kerr, Matty Blair was just unable to reach Danny Parslow's flick-on, and the chance was gone. City were down at the interval once again.

In the second half City pressed for the equaliser, while Mansfield seemed content to soak up pressure, and attack City on the break.

McLaughlin shot wide, for City, Parslow headed wide, and Reedy was far too casual in losing the ball in possession as he was about to shoot.

Wasted chances were costing City dear. On 72 minutes Mansfield hit City on the run as half their players were still up front, and lack of numbers cost the Minstermen another goal. A back-heel from Green (who else), found substitute Aman Verna, and he sent in a rocket from 25 yards to give Ingham no chance. Another mountain to climb.

That old fighting spirit was needed now, and City found it in abundance. James Meredith stormed down the left, and delivered a low cross, which Matty Blair almost stumbled over, but he managed to guide it into the net. There were 13 minutes left.

City stormed on, their tails were up, Matty Blair charged into the box, and the ball fell to Reedy, whose snapshot was incredibly saved by Marriott at full length, but City were not done yet.

Their never-say-die attitude kept them going to the end. In the 90th minute, Danny Parslow was increasingly more involved in the action up front. He found himself heading the ball more in hope than anything else, but luckily it found its way to Jamal Fyfield. The City substitute gloriously composed himself, and chipped the keeper to put City back on level terms from being two down 18 minutes earlier. A brilliant comeback by City once again, but there was hardly time to search for a winner, and they had to settle for yet another draw.

The way it happened, or that's the way it seemed to me at least, it was a point gained rather than 2 points lost, especially against such dangerous opponents.

After City's 9th draw in 13 games (in the Conference), they were down to 5th, and just in the play-offs. Luton Town had taken advantage of their Festive fixtures, against Kettering and had duly thrashed them 5-0 at their place, giving them a 10-1 aggregate against the Poppies, and they were up to 3rd ahead of Southport in

4th, who had been hammered 6-0 at home by rampant Fleetwood. Wrexham were still top having beaten Telford 4-0 at home.

YORK CITY: Ingham, Oyebanjo, Meredith, Kerr, McGurk (Fyfield 32), Parslow, Boucaud, McLaughlin, Henderson, (Reed 55), Chambers (Pilkington 66), Blair.

Subs not used: Moke, Challinor.

MANSFIELD TOWN: J Marriott, O'Neill, Riley, Sutton, Freeman, Roberts (Stevenson), Murray, Howell (Verma), Dyer, Green (Worthington), Meikle.

CITY 2   MANSFIELD 2   Attendance: 4,284.

Scorers: CITY, Blair 77; Fyfield 90   **MANSFIELD,** Green 14; Verma 72.

On January 7th, it was time to go for the double over the struggling Imps at Sincil Bank. To my way of thinking, City were drawing far too many games, and that could cost us our play-off place. Nothing less than 3 points would do at Lincoln.

Reedy started instead of Henderson, and Smithy came in for the injured McGurk to partner Danny Parslow in the middle. Danny Pilkington started as well, and new signing Scott Brown from Fleetwood replaced Boucaud in midfield.

Chances for both sides were few and far between in the first half, and there was hardly a shot in anger, none that I can recall.

City began the second period with just a little more urgency, thank goodness. McLaughlin had the only real chance from a free-kick in the first half, and was instrumental in City's first effort after the interval, with a 12-yard shot which he blazed over the bar. Next, a lob by Pilkington was easily saved by Anyon.

Lincoln seemed content to soak up all the pressure, hardly venturing to go on the attack themselves. On 64 minutes, Matty Blair found himself with just enough room to send his shot past Anyon after Reedy was blocked, and City were ahead at last.

There seemed little danger from Lincoln making a comeback, but really City just got stronger. Debutant Brown, had a shot deflected wide, then Pilkington, running down the left wing provided a perfect cross for Matty Blair to come storming in at pace, and head in from 8 yards to give City a comfortable lead. It was Blair's 7th goal in the last 6 games, and he was having a purple patch.

Lincoln finally made a go of it, but far too late. Challinor got away with a possible hand-ball in the box, and Michael Power had Lincoln's first shot on target. Substitute Jamie Taylor cleared the bar in the dying minutes, but the Imps were doomed. This was City's second double of the season.

City were up to 4th, a point clear of the chasing pack, in advance of the Minstermen's day off League duties next Saturday (it would be FA Trophy time again). Kidderminster had sneaked into 5th spot after beating Hayes and Yeading, and they were looking ominous. Luton beat Newport 2-0 and were 3rd. Wrexham and Fleetwood had not played.

LINCOLN CITY: Anyon, Sinclair, Watson, Williams, Nutter, Platt, (Taylor), Thompson, Christophe, Power, Nicolau (Lloyd), Smith (Pacquette).

YORK CITY: Ingham, Challinor, Meredith, Kerr, Smith, Parslow, Brown, McLaughlin, Reed (Chambers 88), Blair, Pilkington.

Subs not used: Potts, Fyfield, Ashikodi, Musselwhite.

CITY 2   LINCOLN 0   Attendance: 3,048.

Scorers: CITY, Blair 64, 72.

CITY had gone down 1-0 at Salisbury's ground in 2009 and had not enjoyed the experience. Now it was round 2 of the FA Trophy and Salisbury were in the Conference South. In fairness, they had beaten a strong Grimsby side in the previous round.

City were unchanged from the Lincoln victory, and had new striker Matthew Blinkhorn, signed from Sligo Rovers on the bench. Jason Walker was missing his 5th game with that groin injury, or whatever the problem was. City were managing OK without their leading scorer.

And they were. Matty Blair was quickly catching Walker now. On 19 minutes he netted his 11th of the season, and his 7th in as many games, after a Danny Pilkington free kick landed at his feet, 4 yards out, and the ball was fumbled into the net by the keeper. Blair was given the goal.

Two minutes later, Matty grabbed his second of the game. He swooped on to a loose ball and delivered an unstoppable 12 yard shot wide of keeper Simon Arthur to give City a comfortable 2-0 lead.

City were rampant now, and it seemed only a question of how many they would score. The 3rd goal came within 5 minutes, as James Meredith blocked a Salisbury pass, and passed to McLaughlin who went rampaging through the home defence and passed the ball to Reed who arched his shot over the onrushing keeper.

It was like a practise game for City now. McLaughlin, that genius of free-kick takers lived up to his reputation on 34 minutes, and curled a 25-yard kick past the Salisbury wall with the keeper nowhere near it.

Disappointingly City took their foot off the gas, allowing Salisbury a chance or two. They took the second one as Jake Reid broke free and chipped over Ingham from 8 yards. Half-time, Salisbury 1, City 4.

Matthew Blinkhorn made his bow on 66 minutes replacing Reed, and having had a shot on the turn well saved by Arthur, he met a cross from Matty Blair, and powered the ball in the roof of the net, just 4 minutes after coming on. 5-1 to the Minstermen.

Annoyingly City conceded again ten minutes later. Substitute Ashikodi gave away a needless penalty by bringing down Daniel Fitchett in the box when there was no real danger. Jake Reid scored his second from the spot.

Paddy McLaughlin was determined to enjoy his 21st birthday, and unleashed an unstoppable shot from 15 yards to seal a comfortable 6-2 win. It was the first time City had beaten Salisbury in their 7th attempt. The march to Wembley was building momentum.

SALISBURY CITY: Arthur, Ruddick, Webb, Dutton, Brett, Losaano (Kelly), Anderson, Clarke, Adelsbury, Fitchett, Reid.

YORK CITY: Ingham, Challinor, Meredith, Kerr, Smith, Parslow, Brown, McLaughlin, Reed (Blinkhorn 66), Blair (Moke 77), Pilkington (Asikodi 77).

Subs not used: Boucaud, Fyfield.

SALISBURY 2   CITY 6   Attendance: 827.

Scorers: SALISBURY, Reid 36; (pen) 81   **CITY,** Blair 19, 21; Reed 26; McLaughlin 34, 87; Blinkhorn 70.

Wrexham won at Tamworth, in the Conference.

EBBSFLEET would be City's next opponents in the FA Trophy. They were also City's next visitors to the Crescent on January 21st.

So, this was to be a dress rehearsal for the FA Trophy 3rd round encounter. City were unchanged for the 3rd match running.

Straight from the start, City were on the attack. Reed collected a head on from the irrepressible Matty Blair early on, but his shot went wide from just outside the box, but City kept on pressing.

Reedy collected the ball on the right from Kerr, then passed to Pilkington, whose cross should have been cleared by Craig Stone, but he miskicked, and Blair claimed his 13th of the season by gobbling up the loose ball, and City had the lead.

Five minutes later the Minstermen were down to ten men. Scott Brown made a dangerous high challenge on Ram Marwa, and the referee had no real option but to send him packing.

Undaunted, City's ten men still held sway. The only real danger from the visitors being a miss by Pinney who gobbled up Danny Parslow's bad back-pass, and should have netted. Ingham stormed out of his box to avert the danger.

Ebbsfleet brought on an extra striker, Lanre Azeez, who was to influence proceedings straight away. He set up Callum Willock, whose shot was comfortably saved by Ingham. The same striker then had a downward header brilliantly saved by bang-in-form Ingham, to ensure that City kept their slender lead till the break.

But not for long. Another former City man, Neil Barrett first headed over, then, on 50 minutes, the troublesome Nathaniel Pinney nipped in smartly to latch on to Willock's header, round Ingham, and stick the ball in the net. He was very quickly made to rue his over-exuberant celebrations in front of the angry City fans, myself included. He would have been better off heading towards his own supporters to celebrate.

The City players felt the anger too. Within a minute they had regained their lead. Straight from the restart City stormed up front, and Reedy forced Edwards into a save. The ball came back to Reed, who passed to Matty Blair to rifle in his 12th goal in 10 games, and his 14th goal all told. The ten men were in no mood to surrender.

Gary Mills brought on Blinkhorn for Reed a few minutes later, and brought Fyfield on for Pilkington, to make it a 4-3-2 set up with Parslow in midfield and Fyfield at the back. City were coping well with their one man disadvantage.

Midway through the second half, Blinkhorn, Meredith and Blair linked up in a typical passing move by City which ended with the City left-back dinking a beautiful little chip over the startled keeper for his first goal of the season, and the ten men had a 2-goal lead.

Until the 87th minute, when Cameron Willock beat Ingham from 12 yards to give the City fans their usual jittery stomachs for the last few minutes .The gritty Minstermen held on, for what had been a hard-earned victory, having been a man short for 75 minutes of the game.

They had done themselves and their supporters proud. Now for the rematch in the Trophy, set for February the 4th.

City held on to their play-off spot, but only just. Kidderminster were becoming a real nuisance now. They had won at Alfreton, and were hanging to City's coat-tails now. Next up for City was a visit to their Aggborough home.

Elsewhere, nothing changed at the top. Wrexham and Fleetwood won, against Darlington and Kettering (the two clubs in danger of losing their existence ate this level). Those two were out of sight, now. They would fight it out for the title on their own. Luton drew at Southport in a thrilling 3-3 draw, and the Hatters were 3 points ahead of City in 3rd place.

YORK CITY: Ingham, Challinor, Meredith, Kerr, Smith, Parslow, Brown, McLaughlin, Reed (Blinkhorn 59), Blair, Pilkington (Fyfield 59).

Subs not used: Boucaud, Moke, Ashikodi.

EBBSFLEET: Edwards, Howe, Stone, Mambo, Herd (Azeez 36), Marwa, Barrett, Phipp, Pinney, Willock, Enver-Marum.

CITY 3   EBBSFLEET 2   Attendance: 2,973.

Scorers: CITY, Blair 10, 52; Meredith 67   **EBBSFLEET,** Pinney 50; Willock 87.

James Meredith watches the ball go over Edwards for City's third goal.

(Picture The Press, York).

So, it was off to Aggborough on Tuesday night, January 24th, for a game which City dare not lose. To do so would be to allow Kidderminster to climb above them in the table, and put the Harriers 3 points clear of City in the play-off race. Chris Smith and Danny Parslow's rearguard partnership for City would be crucial now. Adriano Moke earned his first League start since September due to Brown's suspension.

City showed no sign of nerve's in the early stages, and Danny Pilkington went close to scoring in the 3rd minute from the edge of the box. Moke made a poor attempt at a clearance shortly afterwards, and Ingham had to be alert to grab the ball in time.

Having seen the electric pace of Kiddie's raids back in December, it was clearly going to be a tough night for City's defence. A lightning raid by Tom Sharpe picked out Nick Wright, who beat Ingham with his shot, but Chris Smith cleared on the line.

Dan Bradley put the ball in the net, but his header was happily ruled offside, and City breathed again. Kidderminster were on top. But for the excellent Danny Parslow City could have been 2 down at the break. First, he blocked a goal-bound shot from Kyle Storer, which had a suspicion of hand-ball about it, and then he got in the way of another effort from Jamie Matt after Smith had made a hash of a clearance as well. City were well relieved to go in on level terms at the break.

For the second half, Gary Mills took off Moke and Reed to be replaced by Boucaud and Blinkhorn, but still the Harriers came at City strongly as expected.

A dangerous header from Wright was saved by Ingham, following a free-kick, and City were managing to hold out.

Even better, in the 52nd minute, McLaughlin was at his tricks again. He swept a delicious cross deep into the box, where Chris Smith was lurking, and the City skipper planted a header down into the corner of the net. Gloriously, City were ahead, and they had cut themselves a bit of slack in a match so crucial to their play-off hopes.

Kidderminster pressed for an equaliser, and Ingham had to be alert to keep out a chip from Anthony Maldon, then Bradley's raking shot from outside the box rattled off the woodwork. City's work was not yet done. Sadly, just 6 minutes from the end, they were beaten at last, and it was a bizarre goal to say the least. Substitute James McQuilken launched a free-kick from 40 yards out. It flew across the area, evading strikers and defenders alike, before finishing up in Ingham's net with no-one touching it.

Far from playing for a more than useful point, City, to their credit pressed for a winner. Matty Blair had a shot blocked, and from the corner, Smithy volleyed over the bar. Smith and Parslow had done their jobs in frustrating the Harriers, and a point was fair reward for City's efforts. It looked like being a valuable point in the grand scheme of things.

It was a good midweek for City, notwithstanding their own result.

Southport lost at Lincoln, and on Wednesday, Luton drew with Mansfield.

Fleetwood won at home, and Wrexham surprisingly lost at Forest Green. City were still in 4th, with Kidderminster sticking to them like a leach in 5th, with the same points, and some 14 goals worse off. It looked like City's goal difference could be worth an extra point this season.

KIDDERMINSTER: Breeden, Sharpe, Williams, Jones, Demetriou, Storer, Bradley, Hendrie (McQuilken), Hankin (Malbon), Matt, Wright.

YORK CITY: Ingham, Challinor, Meredith, Kerr, Smith, Parslow, Moke (Boucaud 46), McLaughlin, Reed (Blinkhorn 46), Blair, Pilkington (Chambers 81)

Subs not used: McGurk, Fyfield.

KIDDERMINSTER 1   YORK 1   **Attendance:** 2,417.

Scorers: KIDDERMINSTER, McQuilkin 84   **CITY,** Smith 57.

DARLINGTON had entered administration in early January, and were in big trouble. Every game was in danger of being their last. Their last game at home to Fleetwood attracted a crowd of 5,638, and a lot more were expected for the visit of the Minstermen on January 28th.

I joined the "Harrogate Minstermen" bus at Boroughbridge, as Darlington was a handy place to get to, for a change. As usual, Pete Moss was driving, and I jumped into the front seat with "Monty" from Pocklington for company.

I had been to the now named "Darlington Arena" for the Cup-tie in 2010. I knew where I was going. John Uttley, Peter's right hand man was dropped off at the ground to buy our tickets and programmes for the match. The rest of us were dropped off down the local pub. We were given to understand that we should make our own way to the ground from there. It was a gorgeous, sunny day, so I went for a stroll on my own.

Three "Darlo" fans were walking to the ground, and I had a friendly word with them. They were actually regular supporters, but they said they were expecting 3 or 4 thousand "extra" fans today. I told them City were bringing close to fifteen hundred, and I wished their club the best of luck in staying afloat.

Once I had located John and Pete near the ground to get my ticket it was getting on for half past two. Some people hadn't managed to get their tickets yet, so I had to wait with Pete until they showed up. We went into the Stadium with 10 minutes to kick off.

Nearly 7,000 had turned up (6,413 to be exact). I had seen fans from Middlesbrough, and Sunderland, and even Leeds before the game, all here to support the Quakers, and what a row they made. This was Darlo's biggest crowd for ages, and it seemed to spur them on.

Darlington had 5 teenagers in their starting line-up, but they certainly had plenty of spirit about them. For some strange reason,

City's spirit and work-rate, and passion for the game had seemed to have deserted them, and they were never in the hunt.

Marc Bridge-Wilkinson stung Michael Ingham into a save in the very first minute, and it was all one-way traffic from there. City never managed to get their passing game going, as Darlington stifled them in midfield. Danny Pilkington was having a nightmare of a game out wide. On the few occasions when he got the ball, he failed to do a real lot with it.

So, City got their just desserts just before half-time. A short corner was taken by Darlington. Rob Ramshaw passed to Bridge-Wilkinson on the edge of the box, who crossed in for Adam Rundle to come running in unchallenged, and drove the Quakers into the lead from close range. The 5,000 Darlington fans, whether regulars, or one-timers, were cheering to the rafters. City were despondent.

This was not supposed to happen. City had been unbeaten in 8 away games since Gateshead, and Darlo were supposed to be struggling. But worse was to come for City.

Moments after the break, things got decidely worse. Andre Boucaud lost the ball in midfield, and Kris Taylor, fed John McReady who went round a startled Danny Parslow, before beating Ingham with a crisp, low drive. Most of the "so-called" Darlington fans had missed the goal. I saw hundreds of them appearing from the bowels of the stadium from the refreshment areas, as they heard the roar when the goal was scored. Most of them hadn't bothered to return to their seats in time for the start of the second half. Fair to say, the queues were longer than normal.

Now, City really had to show some urgency and spirit. Sure enough they did; that second goal was the trigger, which they should not have needed in the first place.

On the hour mark the game turned on its head. Chambers and Reed had entered the fray, replacing Boucaud and the disappointing Danny Pilkington.

Chambers made an immediate impact. City had a corner on the left. Chambers kick was gloriously met by Chris Smith, and it was in the net before the keeper blinked, to wake the substantial following of City fans from slumber.

Amazingly, within a minute, City were back on level terms, as Reed slipped in Chambers, and in a flash, the substitute drove the ball in hard from an angle, and it beat the keeper on his left. City fans delirious, but we wanted more.

After a sensational 60 seconds of action, during which time City recovered to parity from being 2 goals down, the rest of the game fizzled out into an anti-climax. Both sets of supporters wanted more, but neither got it.

McLaughlin had a free-kick saved, and Chambers had a shot off target. For Darlington, Harrison headed over, then McLaughlin had a snap-shot blocked. In the dying seconds Smith headed the resulting corner clean over the bar. Another point, but for me it was 2 points dropped. City simply had to turn these draws into wins, and NOW. Ten draws in eighteen games. It would have to do.

"The Show Must Go On" reverberated round the ground as the Tannoy blared it out. Nobody knew which direction City or Darlington would be going on from here.

Thankfully for City, closest rivals Kidderminster lost at Stockport. Luton scraped a 1-0 win at home to Alfreton, and were 5 points ahead of City now. Wrexham and Fleetwood both won, as usual. Out of sight.

DARLINGTON: Pickford, Arnison, (Gray), Harrison, Taylor, Brown, Hopson (Gray J), McReady, Bridge-Wilkinson, Ramshaw, Rundle, Bowman.

YORK CITY: Ingham, Challinor, Meredith ,Kerr, Smith, Parslow, Boucaud (Reed 54) McLaughlin, Blinkhorn, (Fyfield 73), Blair, Pilkington (Chambers 54).

Subs not used: McGurk, Potts.

DARLINGTON 2   CITY 2   Attendance: 6,413.

Scorers: DARLINGTON, Rundle 43; McReady 49   **CITY,** Smith 59; Chambers 60.

Peter dropped me off, kindly at my home village on the way back. For that I was eternally grateful.

The League table was looking good for City at the end of January, but more wins were urgently required, in spite of City only losing once in the last nineteen, ten of which were draws.

BLUE SQUARE CONFERENCE TABLE
AT 28 JANUARY 2012 (TOP 10)

1.	Fleetwood T	30	21	6	3	67-33	69
2.	Wrexham	30	21	5	4	55-19	68
3.	Luton Town	31	16	11	4	59-27	59
4.	YORK CITY	31	14	12	5	62-33	54
5.	Kidderminster	31	15	8	8	57-43	53
6.	Southport	31	15	7	9	48-53	52
7.	Grimsby Town	31	15	6	10	62-44	51
8.	Gateshead	31	14	9	8	50-45	51
9.	Mansfield T	30	12	13	5	47-34	49
10.	Cambridge U	30	13	10	7	40-27	49

CHAPTER 9

FEBRUARY 2012: THE ARCH BECKONS

FEBRUARY was here, and the weather was playing its part in City's season now. The FA Trophy match with Ebbsfleet was postponed on Saturday the 4th. The proposed visit to Blundell Park on February 11th, also fell foul of the winter weather.

None of City's play-off rivals had managed a kick in anger during the first two weeks of the month, either. Fleetwood had struggled to draw with Tamworth, but they were well out of City's reach by now.

Finally, on Tuesday, February 14th, Ebbsfleet came to Yorkshire, hoping to take a significant step towards Wembley at our expense.

Gary Mills had been busy in the January transfer window. Apart from securing the services of Scott Brown and Matthew Blinkorn earlier, he now brought in Ben Swallow, a winger from Bath City, Erik Tonne, a Norwegian striker on loan from Sheffield United, and Chris Doig, a no-nonsense defender from Aldershot. All were to make their debut against the Fleet, who once again had former City midfielder Neil Barrett in their squad.

Jason Walker was back in City's line-up for the first time since December, on the occasion of the Trophy replay at Solihull.

Paddy McLaughlin had a couple of speculative shots early on, and Enver-Marum fired wide for Fleet. Swallow, and the returning Walker, combined for Tonne to have a low shot saved. The Norwegian then had a header saved, and McLaughlin's follow up shot went sailing over the bar.

McLaughlin was involved with nearly everything. Two more attempts failed to find the net, one goal-bound effort blocked, and another went wide.

Ebbsfleet had their chances. First a free-kick from Enver-Marum, deflected wide, and right at the end of the half when a drive by Gozie Ugwu was easily saved by Ingham.

City's first attack of the second half was clinical and decisive. Walker made a teasing cross from the left which evaded Kerr as he attempted to nudge it over the line, but Matty Blair was there to pounce, and nudged the ball in at the far post. The quarter-finals beckoned now.

It wasn't always plain sailing for City after that. At least Mr Pinney wasn't celebrating too much this time. His partner Enver-Marum caused City a few problems though. First he was given a clear run on goal, after a mistake by new boy Doig, and later on, a decent effort, by the former Crawley striker came to nought.

Our friend Mr Pinney was substituted on 80 minutes to ironic applause from some sections of the Shippo, and Callum Willock blazed over with only Ingham to beat.

Sadly for Jason Walker he ended his comeback on a low note. Matty Blair (otherwise now referred to as "Forrest Gump" for his non-stop running) was tripped in the box, and City's now equal top scorer hit the post from the penalty spot.

It did not matter. City were in the quarter-finals, and dreaming of Wembley once again.

YORK CITY: Ingham, Challinor, Meredith (Parslow 84), Kerr, Smith, Doig, Tonne (Chambers 64), McLaughlin, Walker, Blair, Swallow (Reed 63).

Subs not used: Pilkington, Blinkhorn.

EBBSFLEET: Edwards, Stone, Lorraine, Mambo, Howe, Ugwu, Marwa, Phipp, Pinney (Shakes), Willock, Enver-Marum.

CITY 1   EBBSFLEET 0   Attendance: 1,419.

Scorer: CITY, Blair 48.

After a 3-week break from Conference action, Stockport County came to the Crescent on February 18th, looking for revenge after their home defeat by City in October.

Another new signing for City, Ben Gibson, on loan from Middlesbrough, made his debut at left-back, in place of Meredith. Scott Brown returned at the expense of Andre Boucaud, who had sadly deserted to join Luton, in search of promotion success with the Hatters. Ah well. Big shame.

The game started slowly. The first half was mainly a midfield battle of attrition. City were foxed by the way that County crammed the middle of the park to try and stifle their passing game. It worked, in the main.

City were limited therefore to long range efforts from Chambers and Blair, and an off-target header from equal-top-scorer Blair as well. Things were not working out well for the Minstermen.

The second half was even worse for City. After 52 minutes, Smith was beaten in the air by Tom Elliott, and somehow Danny Rowe escaped his markers, and found the room to fire in past Ingham to put City behind at home yet again.

City were malfunctioning. Gary Mills had to do something about it. Hauling off not just one, but two top goalscorers, in Walker and Blair, midway through the second half did not go down too well with City's faithful. That was no surprise, as they had netted 30 goals between them, notwithstanding the massive other contributions they had made this season.

On came Blinkhorn and Reedy instead.

The man from Sligo did make an impression early on, heading against the post from a Chambers corner, and from another corner his header was saved by Ormson. Ten minutes from time, he set up a chance for Ben Swallow which was blocked, and Gibson's header went over the bar. Six minutes to go, and City appeared doomed. But they were not. Jon Challinor launched a "Rory Delap" throw clean across the box which evaded everybody at the near post, but found its way to Reedy, who crashed it in with glee from eight yards out. Glory be, the boss's substitutions had finally paid off to give City a point, we thought.

Five minutes of injury time was announced. In the last minute of the five, Scott Kerr screwed his shot wide from 12 yards out, and that was that, surely. As the Sixth minute of added time was starting (I was timing it on my watch as well, sad person that I am), City were given a last ditch corner.

Paddy McLaughlin launched it deep into the box, Reedy tried an overhead kick, which bounced up to Matthew Blinkhorn, and he gloriously headed in past the keeper to signal general euphoria in the Shippo end, and the other home segments of the ground. Glory be, City had got out of jail in added time to added time, and just how vital could those 3 points be in the long term. We were jubilant, but you had to feel for Stockport County at the timing of the winner.

If this was not a "Fish and Chips" moment, then I would like to know what is.

Gary Mills was hailed as a genius for his brilliant and inspired substitutions, and time would surely tell you that he was.

It just goes to show what a wonderful squad the City boss had at his disposal, and the never-say-die attitude they had that was their recipe for success. There were still 14 nerve-racking League games remaining.

City's "miracle" victory had put them 3 points clear of Grimsby and Kidderminster in 6th and 7th spots, but both of them had a game in hand on the Minstermen, it was a heck of a good job City did manage to take maximum points that day. Luton Town had a comfortable 3-0 win over Tamworth to extend their own unbeaten run to 13 games. They were a worrying 5 points ahead of City in 3rd.

YORK CITY: Ingham, Challinor, Gibson, Kerr, Smith, Doig, Brown (Swallow 60), McLaughlin, Walker, (Blinkhorn 66), Chambers, Blair (Reed 67).

Subs not used: Parslow, Tonne.

Jamie Reed levels the scores in the 84th minute after coming on as a substitute.

(Picture The Press, York).

STOCKPORT: Ormson, Halls, O'Donnell (Piergianni), Connor (Whitehead), Holden, McConvllle, Nolan, Turnbull, Mainwaring (Cole), Elliott, Rowe.

CITY 2   STOCKPORT 1   Attendance: 3,570.

Scorers: CITY, Reed 84; Blinkhorn 90+6   **STOCKPORT,** Rowe 52.

THE following Wednesday was a time for everyone to calm down once again after the euphoria of the weekend. It was time to face the TV cameras at the Crescent once again, this time for the visit of the "Heed" from Gateshead.

Gateshead's hat-trick destroyer of City in September Jon Shaw was again in their starting line up, together with ex-City midfielder Phil Turnbull, who never got a mention last time out.

City's Big Match stage fright loomed its ugly head immediately, and it was a case of "after the Lord Mayor's show" just 2 minutes into the game. From an early corner, Yemi Odubade found Micky Cummins in open space, and the Heed midfielder rattled home a rasping drive which finished up in the back of the net after a slight deflection off Scotty Kerr. The danger signs were there for City.

The ever dangerous Shaw had a shot blocked, after the lively Alan O'Brien had skipped past Jon Challinor as though he wasn't there.

Jason Walker, still searching for his first goal since his comeback, then fired wildly over from 15 yards out. City were going to struggle once again to get anything from this game.

Efforts from Chambers and Blair late in the half, also came to nothing, as City searched in vain to get back in the game before the break.

Jon Shaw showed that he was human, as he prodded a weak effort wide from eight yards out, but that was only a foretaste of what was to come. Just before the hour mark Odubade's brilliant cross from the right flew across to Cummins, and he headed home, unchallenged for his second of the match to put City in dire straits with half an hour remaining.

They had recovered from such a deficit against Mansfield, but Gateshead was a Tyne Bridge too far for City. Reedy did manage to reduce the deficit on 65 minutes, as he headed in McLaughlin's perfect corner, but City's efforts after that were quelled at every stage.

The Heed were our new "Nemesis" by now, having done the double over disappointed City, and they were fleeing back North up the A1 with the precious points in the bag.

City's first defeat in 8 League games had not hurt them quite so badly. Thankfully for the Minstermen, Luton Town had also lost, the previous evening at Barrow, and Wrexham won at Kidderminster, so City were still hanging on to their precious play-off spot.

YORK CITY: Ingham, Challinor, Gibson, Kerr, Smith, Doig, Brown (Swallow 63), McLaughlin, Walker (Blinkhorn 64), Chambers (Reed 64), Blair.

Subs not used: Meredith, Parslow.

GATESHEAD: Deasy, Baxter, Curtis, Clark, Rents, Turnbull, Gate, Cummins, Odubade (Moore), Shaw, O'Brien (Marwood).

CITY 1   GATESHEAD 2   Attendance: 2,683.

Scorers: CITY, Reed 65   **GATESHEAD,** Cummins 2, 57.

SATURDAY, February 25th was FA Trophy quarter-final day at Blundell Park. The Mariners were creeping up the table, and were sitting menacingly in 6th, just 3 points behind City with a game in hand.

But that mattered not on this particular occasion. This game was about dreaming of that Wembley Arch again. After losing there twice in two years, City were dreaming of going to Wembley and winning. Both sides were just two wins from Wembley.

It was a lively opening with City pegging Grimsby back in their own half for long periods, but the first chance came to the dangerous Liam Hearn for Grimsby whose shot had warmed the hands of Michael Ingham, before Mariners full back Conor Townsend did likewise from a set-piece.

Hearn, the Conference Player of the month for January, was a handful. Another shot was bundled wide by Ingham, and then another decent shot was pushed on to the post by the City keeper.

City had their chances, and both Walker and Blair had blazed wide. Ashley Chambers, who had played for Grimsby brought a decent save from keeper McKeown as half-time approached, goalless.

Grimsby came back stronger in the second half, but the gritty City's determination kept them at bay, as the game went into the last 10 minutes, the Minstermen would be happier with a replay.

There was no need for that. A strange and wonderful thing then happened with just 7 minutes left. Scotty Kerr for all his energy and work-rate had never scored for City. Suddenly, the little midfield general found himself in oceans of space, and headed in past a bewildered keeper. It must have been amazing to behold.

City held on for another hard-earned win against a very useful side indeed.

Of the three other semi-finalists, Luton Town, Newport, and Wealdstone, there are no prizes for guessing which one City landed. They come from Bedfordshire, and play in Orange Shirts!! Wembley was just 180 minutes away, but there was a huge obstacle in the way.

GRIMSBY TOWN: McKeown, Silk, I'anson, Pearson, Townsend, Church (Wood), Disley, Thanoj, Coulson (Makofo), Hearn, Duffy.

YORK CITY: Ingham, Oyebanjo, Gibson, Kerr, Smith, Doig, Meredith, McLaughlin (Challinor 83), Walker (Blinkhorn), Chambers, Blair (Moke 72).

Subs not used: Parslow, Reed.

GRIMSBY 0   CITY 1   Attendance: 3,662.

Scorer: CITY, Kerr 83.

February was over. March would pitch City against their renowned enemy Luton no less than 3 times in that month. It would be a month which would go a long way to deciding City's destiny this season.

Whilst City were off duty in the Conference, worrying things were going on. Southport won at Ebbsfleet, and "nicked" City's 4th place spot. Even worse, the dangerous Kidderminster had also won, at Bath, and they had joined City on 57 points. Another worrying thing was Mansfield's surge up to 7th in the table. They had hammered Darlo 5-2 in midweek, and beaten Tamworth on Saturday. They were 2 points behind City as February ended,

BLUE SQUARE NATIONAL CONFERENCE TABLE
AT 28 FEBRUARY 2012 (TOP 10)

1.	Fleetwood T	34	24	7	3	80-37	79
2.	Wrexham	33	23	5	5	60-21	74
3.	Luton Town	33	17	11	5	62-28	62
4.	Southport	34	17	7	10	53-56	58
5.	YORK CITY	33	15	12	6	65-36	57
6.	Kidderminster	34	16	9	9	60-46	57
7.	Mansfield T	33	14	13	6	54-38	55
8.	Grimsby Town	32	16	6	10	64-45	54
9.	Gateshead	33	15	9	9	53-48	54
10.	Barrow	34	15	7	12	53-48	52

CHAPTER 10

MARCH 2012: BRING ON THE LUTON

HAYES AND YEADING do not have a ground of their own. City had beaten them 4-2 at their Woking home in front of 525 spectators in October. It was essential that City do the same again at Bootham to keep a foothold in the play-offs. Ben Gibson came to join his fellow newcomer Doig in the centre of City's defence as Smith was out, suspended, and it seemed unlikely that McGurk would be fit again this season.

City's early season panache and stylish passing seemed to have deserted them, since the departure of Boucaud to those men from Bedfordshire (who we should not need to name by now). They struggled to come to terms with the visitors organised approach for well over half an hour into the game. We, the Shippo-Enders were frustrated.

Hayes and Yeading had the better chances. Julian Owusu sliced his shot wide, then missed a header at the far post. Michael Thalassitis, on loan from Stevenage failed to make Ingham save, and Mark Bentley also had a header wide.

City had an almighty scare when Yassih Moutouakil hit Ingham's post with a speculative cross-cum-shot. They needed to get a grip on themselves, or their season would be going down the pan.

Chambers did manage a couple of chances before the break; first his lob was clawed away for a corner then he scuffed a close range effort wide after making a run on the left. City had a lot of work to do.

After the break, good old Scotty Kerr was back to his normal non-goalscoring self, bless his little cotton socks. He managed to end a promising City move by launching his shot clean out of the ground, and another chance was wasted. Our little midfield dynamo was brilliant at passing, and at closing down attacking moves, but shooting was his weakness, poor lad. We wouldn't have it any other way.

It did not matter one iota. Meredith set off on a run down the left, and fed McLaughlin whose cross was perfectly met by Lanre Oyebanjo to hit a first-time volley past the keeper. At last City had their noses in front, and what a relief it was.

Both City's centre backs had been replaced by now, with various injuries, and Parslow and Oyebanjo were left to perform their duties in the back four. City were getting desperately short of centre-backs by now.

Nothing much came from the visitors to bother them, thankfully, and City seemed on course for victory, and a crucial one. Hayes Dan Spence was sent off for a second bookable offence, and that eased City's nerves for sure. Matthew Blinkhorn headed on to Walker who was brought down by the keeper. Walker finally netted his 16th goal of the season from the spot, and the points were in the bag. Thank goodness.

Luton beat Bath at home. Kidderminster lost at home to Barrow, and Southport drew with Newport. Things were looking brighter, as March rolled on. City were back in 4th. Mansfield kept on plugging away; they won 2-1 against Lincoln, and were becoming a major worry now.

YORK CITY: Ingham, Oyebanjo, Meredith, Kerr, Gibson (Parslow 23), Doig (Moke 60), Challinor, McLaughlin, Walker, Chambers (Blinkhorn 83) Blair.

Subs not used: Reed, Pilkington.

HAYES and YEADING: Arnold, Moutouakil, Cadmore, Walsh, Spence, Hand, Pele (Collins), Bentley (Warren) Williams, Owusu (Wishart), Thalassitis.

CITY 2   HAYES 0   Attendance: 2,603.

Scorers: CITY; Oyebanjo 57, Walker (pen) 90.

TAMWORTH, formerly managed by Gary Mills came back to York after already getting one over their old boss in September, with the help of two spot kicks. They were out to spoil City's party again as the Minstermen faced their second home game out of three inside 8 days.

Parslow and Fyfield came in for the injured Doig and Gibson, in City's revamped back line. Oyebanjo was at right-back and Meredith left.

Jason Walker had not seemed fully fit since his return against Ebbsfleet, to my way of thinking, and many others too. Sadly he limped out of the action yet again after ten minutes, and was replaced by Matthew Blinkorn. No-one knew what the injury was this time.

City huffed and puffed all night. Tamworth failed to trouble Michael Ingham all evening, but City weren't a whole lot better. Tamworth had learned from other sides that the best way to stop City scoring was to stop their engine-room from working, so they worked hard hassling and harrying City in the middle of the park without doing a real lot of attacking themselves.

Ashley Chambers curled a shot wide, and Matty Blair's effort was deflected wide for a corner. City had one scare when Meredith appeared to trip Connor Taylor in the box, but Tamworth had already had more than their fair share of penalties against City this season, thank you very much. Kieron St Aimee shot over the bar, and an effort from Taylor ended up on the roof of the Shippo. Nix curled over a free-kick late in the half. City needed a kick up the backside.

City decided Lanre Oyebanjos missile throw-ins were their best chance of launching attacks. Challinor headed over from one. Blinkhorn headed wide from a corner, but a goal just would not come.

Pilkington fired in a long range shot and Oyebanjo unleashed a rocket, but it all came to nought. Supersub Reedy had duly entered the fray midway through the second half. He had a late attempt kept out by the keeper's legs, and that was almost it.

Injury-time long-range efforts from Oyebanjo and Scotty Kerr were no trouble for the Tamworth keeper, and the Lambs had baffled City once again. A disappointing night for City ahead of Saturday's crucial semi-final clash with you know who !

On Tuesday, Mansfield annoyingly won at Cambridge to join City on 61 points. Luton went down at Wrexham, 2-0 later in the week.

YORK CITY: Ingham, Oyebanjo, Meredith, Kerr, Parslow, Fyfield, Challinor, McLaughlin (Reed 67), Walker (Blinkhorn 11), Chambers, Blair (Pilkington 60).

Subs not used: Potts, Moke.

TAMWORTH: Hedge, Tait, Francis, Green, Habergham, (Barrow), Reece, McKoy, Nix, Thomas, Taylor, St Aimee (Patterson).

CITY 0   TAMWORTH 0   Attendance: 2,249.

NOW for the big one on Saturday. Part one of three.

CITY'S third home fixture of the week was by far the biggest of the lot. There was never going to be any bigger rivalry at this level than the one which had built up in the three years since the Hatters had been unfortunately relegated to the Conference.

The Minstermen had been successful in the 2010 play-off semis at the expense of the Hatters, and had only lost once in the five meetings in the Conference. But all that was History now.

Matty Blair was rested, in favour of Moses Ashikodi who played out wide on the left instead of the 15-goal speedster from Kidderminster. Surprisingly, midfield star Paddy McLaughlin was also sitting on the bench. For some reason, only known to Mr Mills, he started with both Meredith and Oyebanjo in unfamiliar midfield roles.

No matter, everybody was well up for this one. City were lucky not to have lost the rash Ashikodi in the 3rd minute as he recklessly scythed down Charlie Henry. He escaped with just a yellow card.

Ashikodi himself had actually missed a chance in the very first minute, as Luton were on the back foot from the start, well aware of their 3-0 caning last time at the Crescent.

Matthew Blinkhorn's height was causing problems from crosses, he was not exactly an out and out striker, but he had dramatically rescued City against Stockport 3 weeks ago. He was a perfect foil for Reedy, though, and the former City Supersubs combined brilliantly in the 14th minute.

Blinkhorn headed on to Reed, lurking at the far post. Just as he was about to run away in celebration having, unleashed his snap-shot straight into the net, Reed was dismayed to see Jake Howells reach out and "save" it with his hand. Yes, it was a brilliant "save", but it was slightly illegal. Reedy took the responsibility of taking the kick himself, and side-footed confidently to the keeper's left, and City were a goal up with a quarter of an hour gone.

They were also a man up as well. The referee really had no option but to send Howells packing. City had to be in charge from now on. They would really need to go for Luton's throat.

City fans were roaring. This was our big chance to build up a decent first leg advantage now. Blinkhorn and Reed combined again, and Reedy went charging on, but saw his 20 yard shot tipped over by Mark Tyler. Oyebanjo's corner was headed over by Smith.

Ten-man Luton managed to break away sporadically. On one such occasion Greg Taylor had a decent chance after Reed lost the ball in midfield, but mainly it was City who were pressing, with their man advantage. Oyebanjo tried a spectacular overhead kick from a cross by Jon Challinor but Tyler got in the way of it. Ashikodi failed to put away the ball after it fell loose to him.

Annoyingly, Luton had a big chance to level before the break when the towering Jan Kovacs (who had a spell at City) came powering in from a rare corner, beating Challinor to a challenge, but headed wide of Ingham's net. The ten men had survived so far, with just a single goal deficit.

The Shippo-ites were wondering when the second goal was going to come. One was not enough. Reedy was fouled by Keane, who was issued with a yellow card for his pains. Tyler tipped the free-kick over.

Just a minute later, Keane went for a dangerous high tackle on Jamal Fyfield. Many of the City faithful, myself included were waiting to see what happened next, and I, for one had just realised Keane had already been booked a moment earlier. He was off, and that was that. Jubilation in the City ranks. NOW lets go for it.

There were 40 minutes left. City had a two-man advantage. They had to go for more, this was a gift of a chance for City now.

The nine men of Luton were all behind the ball. They simply were determined not to let City past. Ashley Chambers had already replaced the ineffective Ashikodi just after half-time, and young Michael Potts had come on for the injured Oyebanjo just before the Keane dismissal.

Strangely, Gary Mills decided to bring on Danny Pilkington as his final replacement, preferring to leave both Blair and McLaughlin sitting on the bench. Surely, the situation was crying out for Matty's lightning speed, or goodness knows, had Moke been on the bench, he would have delighted in this situation.

City struggled to break down the Luton road-block. They were frustrated time and time again, as Luton intercepted City's passes. Oyebanjo was off the pitch, and Meredith took Fyfield's place, at full back. I think that City really missed McLaughlin's skill, and Boucaud's pretty passing moves, but he was ironically now on Luton's books, though not in the squad today.

Kerr managed to get a shot in, and Blinkhorn had a decent chance saved as well. The City fans were baying for more goals, but they would not come, and time seemed to pass so quickly.

You could almost sense the Luton fans were lapping it all up at the visitors end, as City were getting nowhere fast. In the last

Off you go ! ! ! Luton's Jake Howells handles Jamie Reeds shot on the line.
(Picture The Press, York).

few minutes, Luton's Pilkington's attempted clearance bounced off his team-mate Osano, and Tyler had to produce a brilliant save to keep the ball from going in.

Luton thought they had it in the bag, as the final whistle blew. Yes, there were some moans and groans from City fans. Gary Mills was not downbeat. A win was a win, and that's all that mattered. City were unbeaten on the road since September (in the Conference). One goal advantage was enough for Mr Mills. We hoped it would be enough as well.

Elsewhere, in the Conference, City were pushed down to 6th, as Mansfield won at Tamworth, and Southport won against Telford. City would have to rearrange two games because of their participation in the Trophy semi-finals. We always knew that would be the case.

YORK CITY: Ingham, Challinor, Fyfield, (Pilkington 62), Kerr, Smith, Parslow, Oyebanjo (Potts 53), Meredith, Reed, Blinkhorn, Ashikodi (Chambers 49).

Subs not used: Blair, McLaughlin.

LUTON TOWN: Tyler, Asafu-Adjake, Kovaks, G Pilkington, Taylor, Keane, Lawless, Watkins (Osano), Henry (Blackett), Crow (Woolley), Howells.

CITY 1   LUTON 0   Attendance: 3,365.

Scorer: CITY, Reed (pen) 14.

NOW, it was off to Blundell Park again, for another difficult encounter on Tuesday night.

Jason Walker returned for City, but it was far from certain whether he was fully fit or not. Meredith went back into midfield, with McLaughlin and Blair happily back to starting duties. No doubt some City minds were on the Luton rematch on Saturday, but League points were essential now.

Grimsby's lethal striker Liam Hearn was out, injured, for the Mariners.

City were under the cosh at first. Ingham had to be alert to keep out an Elding header, and then he managed another decent save from a dangerous strike from the same player.

Reedy missed a chance at the far post, and then Jason Walker shot wide following a header on by Meredith.

Hesitancy in the Mariner's defence allowed Reedy to take advantage. He robbed the ball off Conor Townsend, and stuck the ball past James McKeown, putting City 1-0 up in the 19th minute.

Matty Blair had a chance to increase the lead but pulled his shot wide, and then a drive from Grimsby's dangerous Michael Coulson was well saved by Ingham. City had plenty more opportunities to go further ahead, but McLaughlin wasted one glorious opportunity when he was sent clear with just the keeper to beat. Matty Blair had a weak effort at the far post, which he really should have put away, but his recent scoring touch was missing. All in all City had enough chances in the first half to have been well in front.

Two minutes into the second period, a McLaughlin corner was headed on by Meredith, and the keeper parried it away. Chris Smith was lurking, and put away his third goal of the season off his shin. City were 2-up, and looking good.

But not for long enough. Walker missed a golden chance after a lightning raid by Blair had set him up. He fired wide, and kept Grimsby in the game when they should have been dead and buried.

City soon paid for all those chances missed. On 74 minutes, a poor Fyfield clearance fell to Peter Winn, whose cross was met by Elding, who headed in for 2-1.

City were getting frantic now. It seemed inevitable that they would concede again. Seven minutes later, Ingham punched a Townsend cross into the air, and in came Michael Coulson to head in from the angle, and City had lost their two-goal lead.

Enter Jamal Fyfield, that Mr Versatile who pulled City back from 2-0 down against Mansfield in January. Following a last minute corner after Ian Miller had headed wide, he charged upfield from his left-back slot, and caught hold of a perfect rasping drive from the edge of the box to send the ball scorching into McKeown's net, and send the City fans behind the goal into jubilation.

What a squad we had. What a bunch of fighters, what a bunch of spirited, determined lads. I wish I had been there to share the celebrations. That could be a vital, vital win in City's bid for promotion.

For my sins, I should be ashamed of myself. On hearing from Barry Parker that Grimsby had equalised, I turned the radio off, and went outside to search for my unfortunate cat to let him feel the brunt of my substantial annoyance and anger. Happily the cat could not be found.

I had given up. On finally looking at the scores on teletext it is fair to say that I was fairly pleased to see that City had clinched the victory at the death. Silly, stupid faint-hearted me.

City were back in 5th. They were ready for the battle of Kenilworth Road on Saturday in the 2nd leg of the FA Trophy semi-final. The Wembley Arch was beckoning once again.

GRIMSBY TOWN: McKeown, Silk, Pearson, Miller, Townsend, Coulson, Disley, Thanoj (Wood), Winn, Soares (Duffy), Elding.

YORK CITY: Ingham, Challinor, Fyfield, Kerr, Smith, Parslow, Meredith, McLaughlin, Walker (Blinkhorn 80), Reed, Blair.

Subs not used: Pilkington, Brown, Doig, Ashikodi.

GRIMSBY 2   CITY 3   **Attendance:** 4,250.

Scorers: GRIMSBY, Elding 74; Coulson 81   **CITY,** Reed 19; Smith 47; Fyfield 90+3.

It was clear just how vital City's win at Blundell Park had been. Kidderminster went down at Telford, while Luton scrambled a late, late draw at Darlington (in front of 1,382 spectators). Mansfield drew at home to Fleetwood, and Southport drew at home to lowly Kettering. City were hanging on in there.

SATURDAY, March the 17th was the day of the FA Trophy semi-final, second leg at Kenilworth Road, Luton. Here we go again.

I, myself was off to see my best pal Ted, at his Poppleton abode. We planned to listen to the Radio commentary of the match, and have a cup of tea or two.

I arrived with 5 minutes to spare, and we tuned in to Barry Parker and Chris Jones, to see what they had to say.

City had McLaughlin, Walker, and Blair back in the side from missing out on the first leg victory. A large, vociferous crowd of nearly 6,000 (all except for 400 clad in orange) were well up for it, as we of course were in the first encounter.

City's lead was slender, but they seemed quite content to soak up Luton pressure early on. The danger signs were there for City. Stuart Fleetwood collected a pass from Alex Lawless, the former City favourite, but he fired wide of Ingham's goal. Following that, George Pilkington's header was saved by Ingham, and Lawless's shot was blocked.

As expected, it was all Luton now. Danny Crow had a crisp shot, saved by Ingham after he had spun round on a sixpence, and then another Fleetwood effort, finished high and wide in their next attack. City were on the back foot now.

Following a heavy challenge from Keith Keane, who had been sent off in the first leg (how come he was allowed to play in the second leg, I wonder), poor Scotty Kerr was struggling midway through the first half. Sadly our brilliant little midfield General had to hobble off, to be replaced by Scott Brown. That was a major blow for City, and it seemed that Kerr may be out for the remainder of the season.

Inevitably, the Luton pressure went on and on, and inevitably they found the net just before half-time. Winger Robbie Wilmott collected a wicked cross from Danny Crow on the right, and he gobbled up the chance before Ingham reached it. Fair enough, it was probably deserved on the balance of play in the first period. All to play for now; the sides were level.

City had to take the game by the scruff of the neck, there was no point being negative now. Chambers came on for the tiring Walker, and this certainly gave City far more mobility up front. The substitute just cleared the Luton crossbar moments after coming on, and then he volleyed tamely at the keeper later on.

And then he had a glorious chance to send City through. Running clear of the last defender, Chambers had the goal at his mercy, but somehow he managed to drag his shot wide, and a big chance had gone.

City seemed edgy, and conceded a couple of free-kicks. First, Willmott forced Ingham into a save, then the same player curled his shot wide after a dangerous run.

As extra-time approached a volley by Danny Crow was deflected over the bar. It seemed like both sides had settled for the extra period.

Then gloriously, and suddenly (we heard), a delicious cross by Fyfield came across, and Matty Blair came charging in to meet it perfectly and head it into the Luton net. Delirium amongst the near-400 City fans who had braved the journey down. Well played to every one of those supporters after what happened in 2010.

Matty Blair heads home the 90th minute winner to break Luton hearts.

(Picture The Press, York).

Luton were on their knees in abject misery. The old enemy had done them once again. They did have one dramatic penalty appeal turned down in stoppage time, but they knew the game was up.

Well, my friend Ted, we're off to Wembley once again. For some strange reason it all felt so normal, as if we expected that's the way it would always be.

Gary Mills was right. He always felt that City would manage to avoid defeat at Kenilworth. Wembley here we come. The third time in 4 years.

Ted and I had another cuppa. It was time to start planning for our next visit to the Wembley Arch on May the 12th.

The cat was waiting when I got home. He was a lucky cat today.

With the euphoria of reaching Wembley once again, City had to be a bit concerned about events in the Conference. Kidderminster won at Braintree, but more significantly for us, Southport had thrashed Stockport 5-0 to leapfrog City into 5th, and Mansfield had stormed into 3rd place out of nowhere, having marmalised Barrow 7-0 to continue their fantastic run. City were now 6th, and although they were basking in FA Trophy glory, there was a lot of work to do in their last 10 games in the League. No less than 6 of which were away from home.

LUTON TOWN: Tyler, Osano, Kovacs, G Pilkington, Taylor, Willmott, Keane, Lawless, Howells, Fleetwood, (Watkins), Crow.

YORK CITY: Ingham, Challinor, Fyfield, Kerr (Brown 24), Smith, Parslow, Meredith, McLaughlin, Walker (Chambers) 46, Reed (Blinkhorn 90), Blair.

Subs not used: Musselwhite, Doig.

LUTON 1   CITY 1   Aggregate: 2-1 CITY   Attendance: 5,796.

Scorers: LUTON, Willmott 43   **CITY,** Blair 90.

If ever there was a six-pointer this was surely it. Fifth placed Southport were coming to the Crescent. It was a match we dare not lose.

Surprisingly to some, Gary Mills selected three defenders in City's midfield for the game, namely Oyebanjo and Meredith, who had played there before, and recent newcomer, Ben Gibson, whose remit, was to block, and be the anchor man in place of the injured Scotty Kerr. Even Paddy McLaughlin was left on the bench again, perhaps being less than fully fit.

The new-fangled City Engine room spluttered and stuttered through the first half, and to be honest the Minstermen failed to make much headway against a superbly organised and determined Southport side, who had been the surprise package in the Blue Square this season.

Andy Owens missed a decent chance to put the Seaside team ahead after only 5 minutes when he fired wide of Ingham's near post. Then Reed and Meredith combined to set Matty Blair on one of his speedy runs, but he curled his shot well wide as well. Midway through the half, Reedy back-heeled into the net, but the offside flag was raised. It was a very close call by all accounts. Otherwise the stubborn trio of Southport centre-backs kept City at bay easily for the rest of the first period.

Southport's confidence was growing, now, the more ineffective City were. In the 65th minute the ball was carelessly given away by Matty Blair, allowing Gray to send Andy Owens clear. The full-back turned striker fired confidently past Michael Ingham, and City were down at home for the third time, in the last five games.

Just four minutes later, things got far worse. Reverted full back again, Ben Gibson challenged Russell Benjamin on the half-way line, leaving both players in a heap on the floor. It certainly appeared to me that the rest of City's team had stopped, presuming the referee would halt proceedings. He didn't do that, and Southport took full advantage of the situation, Owens finding Gray, who cut inside before beating Ingham for a 2-0 lead. City seemed unjustly done by, but there was nothing they could do about it.

City had never been beaten by a 2-goal margin all season, and, true to form, they fought back well. Six minutes from time, Reedy turned swiftly on the edge of the box, and delivered an unstoppable shot past Tony McMillan for his 12th goal of the season.

Sadly, it was too little, too late. City had been "mesmerised" by Southport's second, and they had left themselves too much to do this time.

Moke's first appearance off the bench in 5 games almost changed things. He teed up Blair perfectly in the dying moments, but City's speedy winger side-footed agonisingly wide from four yards out, and that was that.

It really seemed to me that City's play-off hopes were in grave, grave doubt right now. I picked my programme up off the floor.

City were down to 6th now, 3 points off the play-offs but with 2 games in hand on Southport, who were 5 points up on City. Mansfield's fantastic run came to an end at Fleetwood as they lost 2-0, but they were well ensconced in 3rd place now. Luton dropped 2 points at home to Grimsby, while Kidderminster were still lurking just below the play-off slots after a comfortable 3-1 win over Darlington, in the end.

YORK CITY: Ingham, Challinor, Fyfield (Moke 56), Gibson (McLaughlin 78), Smith, Parslow, Meredith, Oyebanjo, Reed, Chambers (Blinkhom 79), Blair.

Subs not used: Brown, Doig.

SOUTHPORT: McMillan, Smith, Akrigg, Davis, Grand, Lever, Benjamin, Parry, Gray, (Carden), Ledsham, Owens.

CITY 1   SOUTHPORT 2   Attendance: 3,465.

Scorers: CITY, Reed 84   **SOUTHPORT,** Owens 65; Gray 69.

EVEN in the Blue Square National Conference there are no easy games, especially at such a crucial time of the season as this. Bath City were almost down and out at the bottom of the table, but City had struggled to beat them at the Crescent in September.

The Minstermen had a job to do, and nerves would soon be coming into the equation at the end of March. For City, Doig came in for Parslow, and McLaughlin regained his midfield berth.

Matty Blair had seemed to have left his scoring boots at home again. After netting 12, in 11 games over the New Year period, he was misfiring now. Twice he had early opportunities to ease City's nerves in a match they had to win, and twice he failed. First, his shot was comfortably saved on 3 minutes, and then he drove over the bar, when a couple of months ago it would have bulged the net.

The more times City missed their chances, the more the confidence of Bath players grew. Scott Murray missed a decent chance for them as City's early dominance faded. Jamie Cook headed wide from a Canham cross and it was 0-0 at the break.

Thankfully the Minstermen had more urgency as the second half began. McLaughlin was fed by Reedy, and the re-instated midfield ball-player fired in an angled drive past Glyn Garner for his 11th goal of the season to ease the City men's nerves.

Reedy missed another chance on a one-to-one with the keeper and then Scott Murray went close for Bath from 20 yards following a cross from Watkins.

Chance after chance came and went for the Minstermen, and chance after chance went begging. Reed's header was easily saved, and then Jon Challinor hoisted a shot from 8 yards over the bar. Blair messed up again, shooting straight at Garner, and Oyebanjo, then Reed, again drove wide after a breakaway raid by City. The Minstermen should have put the game to bed by now.

They very nearly paid the ultimate price for all those missed chances. Right at the very death, there was a scramble in the box, and Watkins back-heeled the ball towards the net. Officially it was cleared by Oyebanjo on the line, but many in the ground, including Mr Barry Parker thought it was a goal. Personally my nerves could take no more. I was in bits by the end, and had not a single finger-nail left.

That was a very, very close call for City. Goodness only knows how they would have got over losing 2 points there, especially with another crucial visit to Kenilworth Road just 3 days away.

Southport drew at Braintree. City were 3 points behind the Seasiders with a game in hand. City were gloriously ahead of Luton Town on goal difference prior to their next titanic battle with the Hatters.

BATH CITY: Garner, Simpson, Preece, Burnell, Gallinagh (Watkins), Murray (Hogg), Connolly, Canham, Russell, (Egan), Cook, Stonehouse.

YORK CITY: Ingham, Challinor, Meredith, Brown (Parslow 78), Smith, Doig, Oyebanjo, McLaughlin, Reed (Blinkhorn 90), Chambers (Moke 84), Blair.

Subs not used: Bopp, Tonne.

BATH CITY 0   CITY 1   Attendance: 565.

Scorer: CITY, McLaughlin 50.

So, for the third time in the month of March, it was time to face the Hatters once again, on a Friday night, and the game was once again being televised live. That was all that City needed, bearing in mind their abysmal record on the telly.

I was all set to watch the game on the big screen at a local pub in Boroughbridge, having been assured that they would be screening it. My evening's entertainment (if that's what you want to call it) was cruelly curtailed before it had begun. I wondered why none of the local City fans were in the bar as I arrived at just before kick-off. No wonder, the poor landlord (it wasn't his fault) had not realised the Channel it was on had not been subscribed to. It was my fault, I should have been more specific in my telephone conversation on the night before. I waited till the kick-off was due, in case the pictures stayed on the screen after the match started. I was hoping for a miracle really. The picture was scrambled when the match began and I was snookered. I did see some of the build-up though.

I wasn't very happy with myself. Apologising to the landlord, I was off like a bullet, speeding back home on my clapped-out bike. I was pretty sure that City would be losing when I got home. Sadly that's the pessimist in me. I somehow felt that this was Luton's turn to beat the City, they were a very useful side at home. I should have more faith in the lads by now. Sorry.

Well, City were behind, as I reached home after 15 minutes of the game. I found out that Andre Gray had put the Hatters ahead in the 5th minute, after beating Smithy in a challenge, and that he should really have made it two just before I made it home. Seemed like City were suffering the backlash from their recent success in ending Luton's hopes of getting to Wembley, just 13 days ago. It seemed like Luton's day for revenge had arrived at last. I hoped not.

I had to be content with my old friend the radio, and Mr Parker and Mr Jones being my eyes once again. I don't know whether it would be any less nervous if I had managed to see the pictures for myself. A Gibson tackle stopped Alex Lawless in his stride, then Jan Kovacs Luton's other former Minsterman headed wide from a corner.

City had three decent chances before the break. Jamie Reed shot straight at Tyler, and then Lanre Oyebanjo hit the post, and McLaughlin sliced wide just before half-time.

I didn't know what to do with myself, I was all over the place with nerves. I listened on till midway through the second half. Andre Gray was gifted a golden chance in front of goal, but thankfully shot straight at Ingham. McLaughlin then set up Reedy whose shot was saved by Tyler, then a curling shot from Meredith sailed over the bar.

A 40-yard lob by Oyebanjo was scrambled over by a grateful Mark Tyler, as City battled on to try and save a point.

I have to be totally honest at this point. I did something that I happened to do once before in previous seasons (when City were playing at Droylsden, some 4 years ago, and it worked) I decided that my nerves could take no more. There was absolutely no disrespect for City ever intended, it was just that I figured that if I wasn't listening to the commentary, it was usually a sign that City would go and put one in the net. I turned off the radio with some 12 minutes to go, hoping and praying that City would produce the goods for me. I would turn on the telly after the final whistle went, or sneakily put the radio back on in a few minutes time if I was brave enough.

We all know full-well exactly what did happen next. Moments after my radio silence began, City substitute Eugene Bopp, making his debut, passed the ball to Paddy McLaughlin from a free-kick, and he drove the ball gloriously into the net for City's equaliser. How spooky was that; I had switched off just a minute or so earlier.

And we all know what happened after that, on what was a glory night for City. Six minutes later, a stinging drive from Ashley Chambers was saved by Tyler. Gloriously, James Meredith slotted in the rebound for yet another famous City victory over the Orange enemy. It must have been majestic for the near-200 strong band of City fans who had made the journey there. It must have felt like the Minstermen were really in contention for the play-offs now. It must have felt for Luton fans that they were destined never to beat City again, and it must have seemed to them that they wouldn't even make the play-offs at that point in time.

The Hatters fans were screaming for the head of manager Gary Brabin. As it turned out, they would get their wish. Paul Buckle, the ex-Torquay manager had already been lined up to replace him, so I understand, and he was given the job as was predicted.

And I had missed it all. It served me right. I did not know whether to laugh or cry when I sneaked the radio back on as added time was being played. I was astounded, but obviously totally delighted when Barry Parker said that City were hanging on to their lead. I could not believe it but it was true. Even as I listened to the dying seconds of added time I was more nervous than I ever was before, but gloriously, City hung on for 3 massive points.

City were up to 4th, and 3 points clear of the Hatters now. With just 7 games to go, their fate was in their own hands now. I'm not sure if my nerves could take much more.

LUTON TOWN: Tyler, Osano, G Pilkington, Kovacs, Howells, Lawless, Keane, Poku (Watkins), Willmott, Crow (McAllister), Gray (Fleetwood).

YORK CITY: Ingham, Challinor (Bopp 68), Gibson, Oyebanjo, Smith, Doig, Meredith, McLaughlin (Parslow 90), Walker, Reed (Chambers 64), Blair.

Subs not used: Moke, Blinkhorn.

LUTON 1   CITY 2   Attendance: 5,925.

Scorers: LUTON, Gray 5   **CITY,** McLaughlin 80; Meredith 86.

On the Saturday I followed the Conference scores on-line. Kidderminster had really annoyed me by snatching a last-minute winner at Grimsby, but, by the same token Southport were beaten by Hayes with a last gasp goal as well. City stayed in 4th place at the end of March.

BLUE SQUARE NATIONAL CONFERENCE TABLE AT 31 MARCH 2012 (TOP 10)

1.	Fleetwood T 41	30	8	3	98-41	98
2.	Wrexham 40	28	6	6	76-26	90
3.	Mansfield Town 41	20	14	7	74-46	74
4.	YORK CITY 39	19	13	7	74-41	70
5.	Southport........................ 41	20	10	11	63-60	70
6.	Luton Town.................... 39	18	13	8	67-37	67
7.	Kidderminster................. 41	19	10	12	71-55	67
8.	Grimsby Town................ 41	18	10	13	75-57	64
9.	Gateshead 40	18	10	12	61-56	64
10.	Forest Green. 41	16	13	12	59-42	61

Squeaky-Bum time coming.

CHAPTER 11
APRIL 2012: "SQUEAKY-BUM" TIME

THE MONTH of April was traditionally-known as "Squeaky Bum" time as Sir Alex Ferguson famously once said.

Newport County had defeated Wealdstone in the other Trophy semi-final, and they would be City's opponents at the famous Arch on May the 12th. First they had to meet City twice in the Conference in the next 11 days. The Welshmen were also desperate for points in their bid to avoid the dreaded drop.

For City, on the Tuesday night of April the 3rd, Matthew Blinkhorn and Jamal Fyfield had replaced the ailing Jason Walker, and skipper Chris Smith in the City starting eleven. Danny Parslow also came in to replace Chris Doig at the back. City were unbeaten in 13 games on the road, and had won 3 in a row on their travels. Both sides were obviously nervy with play-offs and relegation at stake, and the bobbly pitch probably did not lend itself to the passing game City had enjoyed for much of the season.

Chances were therefore few and far between in a cagey opening period. Jon Challinor's long range shot was the only chance created in the first quarter of the game, then moments later City won their first corner, but it fizzled out as Blinkhorn was alleged to have fouled Newport keeper Karl Darlow.

City were in trouble just after half an hour. A Newport corner was almost headed into his own net by Danny Parslow. The following corner then cleared Michael Ingham, and it fell to Nat Jarvis who put it in the net to give County the lead.

The Minstermen were stung into action straight away. In a typical show of spirit and determination they were not to be down for long. Lanre Oyebanjo was scythed down outside the box, and

Paddy McLaughlin took full advantage. The resulting free-kick whistled into the net past Darlow's left shoulder, for the Irishman's 13th goal of the season, and City were level at the break.

In the second half, Newport came on strong again. Lee Minshull launched a long range shot which flew over Ingham's bar, before City had another near miss. The Newport keeper dropped Challinor's long throw, but Matty Blair's follow-up shot was blocked.

Twenty minutes from the end, the unmarked Danny Rose turned and shot past Ingham with a raking drive, and City were behind again.

City's battling spirit was still evident, but all their remaining efforts were thwarted. Moses Ashikodi and Adriano Moke replaced Blair and McLaughlin but it was all to no avail. City went down for the first time in 14 away games, and their play-off place was far from certain yet. None of City's rivals were in action that same night.

NEWPORT COUNTY: Darlow, Pipe, Warren, Hughes, Sandell, Minshull, Porter, Foley, Charles, Buchanan (Rose), Jarvis (Reid).

YORK CITY: Ingham, Challinor, Fyfield, Oyebanjo, Parslow, Gibson, Meredith, McLaughlin (Ashikodi 76), Reed (Chambers 64), Blinkhorn, Blair (Moke 76).

Subs not used: Tonne, Bopp.

NEWPORT 2   CITY 1   Attendance: 1,241.

Scorers: NEWPORT, Jarvis 33; Rose 70   **CITY,** McLaughlin 39

TOP SIX STANDINGS

1.	Fleetwood	41	30	8	3	98-41	98
2.	Wrexham	40	28	6	6	76-26	90
3.	Mansfield	41	20	14	7	74-46	74
4.	YORK CITY	40	19	13	8	75-43	70
5.	Southport	41	20	10	11	63-60	70
6.	Luton Town	39	18	13	8	67-37	67

FLEETWOOD, the Blue Square Champions-elect, were next in line to visit Bootham Crescent. That was all City needed after their recent poor run at home. They had only won three times at home in their last eight games. Apart from that, a certain Richard Brodie would be in their side.

I arrived in York much earlier than usual, as a cricket friend of mine was getting married at a Registry Office not far from the ground. As I was waiting to catch a glimpse of him after the Ceremony, hundreds of Fleetwood supporters drifted past on the way to the game.

Being a sociable creature I took my chance and had a chat with some as they were passing by. They were obviously keen to land the title just as soon as possible, and they obviously needed the points just as badly as ourselves. But I took my chance, anyway.

There was a young girl wearing the yellow and black Fleetwood away kit, on the way to the match with her dad. She was around 11 or 12 years old, and said she went to nearly all away games. She was such a chatty little lass, and she knew all there was to know about her team, and others in our League. She seemed to want to offer me some sympathy, as she thought that City would be staying down. Before she continued on her way, the friendly little thing gave me a great big hug, and wished my team good luck. (After today). I had only just met the little girl, but she had made me smile that day.

Other Fleetwood fans were not so gracious. Mostly they reckoned that Wrexham would be the ones to accompany them in going up to the Football League next season. Only time would tell.

Down to business now, and Fleetwood were the favourites. They were 8 points clear of Wrexham with 6 games to go. Chris Doig returned for City, and another newcomer, Eugen Bopp, together with Erik Tonne were brought into a surprise City line-up. Jason Walker was still missing, and Ashley Chambers was on the bench.

Early on, both Tonne and Bopp were both given the opportunity of taking a free-kick each. Both failed to hit the target. New striker Tonne also had a header saved by Davies.

Matty Blair was making one of his trademark bursts into the area, when he seemed to be caught by the boot of Shaun Beeley, but the referee turned a blind eye to it.

Fleetwood's stars were being kept in check, for now. Lee Fowler, their "steal" from Wrexham, was prominent in midfield, while Mangan and Vardy had had a relatively quiet first period. Brodie was still on the bench, and raring to have a go sometime in the second half, no doubt his chance would come.

The first half had been devoid of clear cut chances in a cagey start, but after the break things opened out. The dangerous Vieira had a header wide, and then Lanre Oyebanjo put his wayward shot on to the Shippo roof, after having ran the length of the pitch to meet a Chambers cross.

Chambers then had a chance himself, and forced Davies into a save, then a superb cross from substitute Moke was missed by everyone.

Richard Brodie eventually came on, and replaced another City escapee, Peter Till who had such a quiet first half that no-one realised he was playing. We would notice Brodie more.

And we did. On 73 minutes, that "Angel of the North" found himself in the City box with time and space to spare. We all knew what would happen next, as it was written in the stars.

Brodie despatched the ball past Michael Ingham, and that was that. Fleetwood's title was ever nearer, and City's situation wasn't helped a great deal.

This was the fixture nobody expected York to win. A point would have been handy, however, but it would not come. Moke pulled a good chance wide, then Meredith's downward header was kicked off the line by Fowler.

Matthew Blinkhorn, who had replaced Tonne, came closest of all to levelling, as his header hit the post with two minutes remaining. We all felt that City's performance deserved a point, but instead they went down to their sixth home defeat of the campaign.

Mansfield won at Kettering, and City realised that 3rd place was beyond our reach by now. Should City land a play-off spot they would have a home game first. In the big match at Haig Avenue it was Kidderminster who took the points; they joined City on the 70 point mark. Luton Town lost at Braintree Town, a place where City had to visit last. Things were getting tighter.

YORK CITY: Ingham, Oyebanjo, Gibson, Bopp (Moke 45), Parslow, Doig, Meredith, McLaughlin, Reed (Chambers 65), Tonne (Blinkhorn 76), Blair.

Subs not used: Fyfield, Brown.

FLEETWOOD: Davies, Beeley, McNulty, Pond, Goodall, McGuire, Cavanagh (Vieira), (Seddon 86), Fowler, Till (Brodie), Vardy, Mangan.

CITY 0   FLEETWOOD 1   Attendance: 4,048.

Scorer: FLEETWOOD, Brodie 73.

TOP 8 AT APRIL 7TH

1.	Fleetwood	42	31	8	3	99-41	101
2.	Wrexham	41	28	6	7	76-27	90
3.	Mansfield	42	21	14	7	77-46	77
4.	YORK CITY	41	19	13	9	75-44	70
5.	Kidderminster	42	20	10	12	73-56	70
6.	Southport	42	20	10	12	64-62	70
7	Luton Town	40	18	13	9	68-40	67
8.	Gateshead	41	19	10	12	63-56	67

NOW, it was off to the Derbyshire hills to face up to Alfreton Town. Just City's luck to find the newcomers were in startling form right now. Alfreton had won seven of their last eight games recently, and had virtually ruined Wrexham's title chances at the Racecourse with a 1-0 win there just three days ago.

City needed to get back to winning ways after two straight defeats. It seemed like their play-off destiny would be sorted out in their three remaining fixtures on the road. Moke got his first start since December, and Pilkington returned. Danny Parslow moved into midfield as Meredith reverted to left back.

City had to attack, and they did so from the start. They created four good chances inside the first 10 minutes.

First it was Pilkington, who had a go with a dipping volley, and then a pile driver from Paddy McLaughlin skimmed off the wet surface. Reedy pulled the ball back for Pilkington again, but his shot sailed over the bar, and then the unfortunate Matty Blair's luck was out again. He hit the post from 25 yards. A goal just would not come.

A couple of chances for Alfreton caused City no problems. A volley by Jamie Mullan finished nearer the corner-flag than the target, and Antony Wilson had a free run on goal but Ingham managed to intercept.

Oyebanjo and Meredith both stung the keeper's hands as City kept on coming at the Derbyshire-men, but they could not find that vital goal before the break.

A big chance came and went soon afterwards. Jamie Reed was pole-axed by Darran Kempson, and the penalty was given. Sadly for Reedy his weak shot was easily saved by keeper Stewart, and City battled on.

City were struggling to find a breakthrough, and the City fans who were determined, not to pay for seats were getting ever more drenched by the minute as the rains became torrential.

The chances kept on coming. Moke's long range pass to Matty Blair sent him racing into the box. At long, long last his scoring drought was over. He gave the keeper no chance, and gleefully slotted in his 17th of the season. City were almost home and dry, even if their supporters weren't.

A Derbyshire Monsoon then happened fifteen minutes from the end. The rain was cascading from the skies. Luckily for City, they managed to go 2 up just before the deluge proper came. Lanre Oyebanjo fired in from six yards after McLaughlin had pulled it back for him.

During the last few minutes of the match conditions were becoming farcical, and practically unplayable. Had the rains come down a few minutes earlier the match would certainly have had to be called off. City fans who were there, like my chum Graham told me it was touch and go. He was as drenched as a drowned rat, but he was happy, and so were the dampened band of 720 City disciples.

ALFRETON: Stewart, Law (Deverdics), Kempson, Streete, Franklin, Mullan (Meadows), Moult, Connelly, (Jarman), Brown, Cunnington, Wilson.

YORK CITY: Ingham, Oyebanjo, Meredith, Parslow, Smith (Fyfield), Doig, Pilkington, (Challinor 87), McLaughlin, Reed (Blinkhorn 90), Blair, Moke.

Subs not used: Potts, Tonne.

ALFRETON 0   CITY 2   Attendance: 1,603.

Scorers: CITY, Blair 69; Oyebanjo 76.

I was listening to the radio, and watching the other scores on my computer. I was horrified to see the events at Aggborough as they unfolded. Kidderminster were two down to Newport with four minutes remaining, yet somehow they managed to win 3-2. Had they got a point it would not have bothered City much at all, but the three points kept them hanging on to City's tail, and that was only adding to our nervousness with 4 more games to go. Southport had also sneaked a draw at Barrow but they were almost out of it by now. Luton were still floundering in 7th spot, having beaten Hayes 4-2. They still had 2 games in hand on Kidderminster, and had to meet them at Kenilworth Road yet.

THE TOP 8 AT MONDAY APRIL 9TH

1.	Fleetwood........................ 42	31	8	3	99-41	101
2.	Wrexham 41	28	6	7	76-27	90
3.	Mansfield T..................... 43	22	14	7	79-47	80
4.	YORK CITY..................... 42	20	13	9	77-44	73
5.	Kidderminster................. 43	21	10	12	76-58	73
6.	Southport........................ 43	20	11	12	66-64	71
7.	Luton Town..................... 41	19	13	9	72-42	70
8.	Grimsby Town................ 43	19	11	13	77-57	68

In a titanic encounter at Fleetwood on the following day, Wrexham held the leaders to a 1-1 draw in front of over 4,000 spectators, in the title showdown. Fleetwood now needed two more points to secure promotion.

ON APRIL 14th, things were hotting up. Our FA Trophy Final opponents Newport County were not safe yet, and came to the Crescent for their second dress rehearsal for Wembley, needing points just as desperately as City needed them.

City were unchanged from their victory at Alfreton in the rains, but Jason Walker was on the bench, with Ashley Chambers after both being out of the side for most of the last five games.

City were slow to get out of their traps, and were yet again caught napping early on. This time, Adriano Moke, in only his third start since September had given away a dangerous free-kick which Newport captain Sam Foley launched into the middle for Nat Jarvis to charge in, and head past Ingham.

The men from Wales showed a dogged determination throughout the entire first half, and City found it ever harder scoring first half goals, or any goals, at home. They had only managed one in their last three games at Bootham, and only three times in the first half of the last 17 games.

There were some City chances but nothing came of them. Moke had a speculative shot from outside the box, and then Matty Blair stung the keeper's hands from 20 yards but that was it.

City continued to struggle after the break, but Walker had now entered the fray, replacing Reedy at half-time. Chambers had earlier replaced Moke as well, and Challinor came on for Pilkington.

The visitors were proving a hard nut to crack as their search for vital points continued. They forced a series of corners just after the break.

Enter Jason Walker. The City talisman was showing signs that he was coming back to full fitness ready for the final part of the regular season, happily. He tried an exquisite lob from way outside the box, and saw his shot rebounding off the post.

Moments later, salvation was at hand. Walker hooked the ball over his head, to Chambers, who ran on clean into the box before delivering a return pass to Walker, who despatched it into the net off that same post. The old one-two had worked, and City were back on level terms.

Jason Walker was back to his best, although he missed a couple of half-chances later. Newport had a rare shot from Reid which cleared the bar, and, first Oyebanjo, and then Smith missed good opportunities to secure the victory for the hosts.

A point was not so bad, especially the way it came, together with Walker's pleasing return. We estimated that City would need just 7 more points in the last 3 games to make the play-offs, it would have been all 9 required had we lost to Newport.

With that in mind we were all relieved, and not too disappointed at the end.

Newport were happy with their point as well. I had a word with some of their supporters after the game, and congratulated them on coming all this way. They were joking that if City let them win at Wembley, they would let City win there in the play-off Final a week later. Fair enough, I may have settled for that. We all had our dreams.

YORK CITY: Ingham, Oyebanjo, Meredith, Parslow, Smith, Doig, Pilkington (Challinor 46), McLaughlin, Reed (Walker 46), Blair, Moke (Chambers 37).

Subs not used: Tonne, Gibson.

NEWPORT: Darlow, Pipe, Yakubu, Hughes, Baker (Hatswell), Knights (Rogers), Marshall, Porter, Foley, Reid, Jarvis (Buchanan).

CITY 1   NEWPORT 1   Attendance: 2,824.

Scorers: NEWPORT, Jarvis 4   **CITY,** Walker 59.

Kidderminster had duly clobbered Kettering, 6-1, and that was well expected, and the men from Aggborough leap-frogged City into 4th. Southport drew 2-2 at Tamworth after being two goals up, and were almost goners now. Luton, under new manager Paul Buckle only drew at Alfreton 0-0 where City had succeeded earlier. The last two weeks of the season would be mind-boggling.

TOP 9 PLACINGS AT APRIL 14TH

1.	Fleetwood T 44	31	10	3	102-44	103
2.	Wrexham 43	28	8	7	79-30	92
3.	Mansfield 44	23	14	7	82-48	83
4.	Kidderminster............... 44	22	10	12	82-59	76
5.	YORK CITY 43	20	14	9	78-45	74
6.	Southport...................... 44	20	12	12	68-66	72
7.	Luton Town................... 42	19	14	9	72-42	71
8.	Gateshead 43	20	10	13	64-58	70
9.	Grimsby T 44	19	12	13	79-59	69

It looked like City had no chance of catching Mansfield, in 3rd now, barring a miracle. If City were to make the play-offs it would almost certainly be a home match-up with either Wrexham or Mansfield in the first leg. That was a long way off yet, but City fans were dreaming still.

These were the fascinating remaining fixtures to be played out in the next two weeks; (for City's main rivals)

YORK CITY:	Away	Cambridge Tue Apr 17
	Away	Braintree Sat Apr 21
	Home	Forest Green Sat Apr 28
MANSFIELD TOWN:	Home	Wrexham Sat Apr 21
	Away	Kidderminster Sat Apr 28
KIDDERMINSTER:	Away	Luton Sat Apr 21
	Home	Mansfield Sat Apr 28
LUTON TOWN:	Home	Ebbsfleet Tue Apr 17
	Home	Kidderminster Sat Apr 21
	Away	Gateshead Tue Apr 24
	Away	Fleetwood Sat Apr 28
SOUTHPORT:	Home	Ebbsfleet Sat Apr 21
	Away	Grimsby Sat Apr 28
GATESHEAD:	Away	Bath City Sat Apr 21
	Home	Luton Tue Apr 24
	Home	Telford Sat Apr 28
GRIMSBY TOWN:	Away	Telford Sat Apr 21
	Home	Southport Sat Apr 28

As Luton had to face Kidderminster, the winner would almost certainly end up in the play-offs. That match-up favoured City as points would obviously dropped by someone. Kidderminster had to face Mansfield as well, but you would think by then their 3rd place would be assured. Luton faced tough visits to Gateshead and Fleetwood yet. We did not envy them for that. Southport versus Grimsby may not matter much.

If City were to do it, It seemed like they would have to do it on the road. They were in good spirits after having won four out of their last five outings, after all. Two more wins would put City, into the land of dreams. It was so, so near now.

Cambridge would provide a stern test of City's nerves and mettle on Tuesday night, April 17th. Jon Challinor, Ben Gibson, and importantly Jason Walker, started, but there was a surprise in City's goal.

Michael Ingham had not missed a single one of City's 43 games in the Conference. He was sidelined with a shin injury, and the 43-year old reserve Paul Musselwhite was set to make his first professional start for six years in becoming City's oldest ever player to boot.

Musselwhite's nerves were eased early on when he got his hands on a dangerous cross from Jonathan Thorpe. His hands were warmed again after just 5 minutes as former City striker Michael Gash presented him with a comfortable save.

Chambers shot wide after a classy flick by Walker, and then Lanre Oyebanjo hit his shot into the side netting. Chambers could have done better, moments later. Instead of feeding the lurking Walker, he chose to have a go himself, and had his ambitious shot easily saved.

Cambridge are no mugs at home, and boasted one of the best home records in the league. A couple of long-range shots by Harry Pell failed to trouble Musselwhite, but then City lost a key defender. The injured Chris Doig was replaced by Danny Parslow.

Gash forced Musselwhite into a more difficult save, then Chambers wasted another chance from 25 yards, before City found themselves in a whole heap of trouble before the break.

Ben Gibson had seemed to follow through on a challenge at the edge of the box, on Thorpe, and the referee had no hesitation in brandishing the red card.

It was really backs-to-the wall stuff for City now, with a man down against a really decent side. They needed their fantastic spirit now, in bundles.

And they got it. Even after Lanre Oyebanjo limped off injured to be replaced by Michael Potts on the hour. Moments after that came a subliminal moment in City's glorious season so far.

Young Potts released Jason Walker for a run at goal. City's leading scorer and talisman ran on and swept his angled drive past Naisbitt for his 18th of the season and the City fans were ecstatic.

There were 25 nervy minutes left, but City stretched their every sinew, and their every muscle in their weary bodies to keep the "U's" at bay. This was it, the final furlong now, and they all held their heads high, and they did us all proud, all ten of them.

Paul Musselwhite was jubilant at the end, as was expected. A clean sheet in his first game, and three more than priceless points while playing over half the game with one man short. Such spirit and passion had taken them to the very brink of the play-offs. Bring on Braintree, Saturday. That game could not come soon enough.

Luton duly despatched Ebbsfleet 3-0 at home, to enhance their own play-off chances. For City, it was all about Saturday now.

CAMBRIDGE: Naisbitt, Thorpe (Eaves 46), McAuley, Hudson, Jennings, Hughes, Shaw (Brighton), Jarvis, Pell, Berry, Gash.

YORK CITY: Musselwhite, Challinor, Gibson, Oyebanjo (Potts 60), Smith, Doig (Parslow 19), Meredith, McLaughlin, Walker (Blinkhorn 90), Chambers, Blair.

Subs not used: Reed, Tonne.

CAMBRIDGE 0   CITY 1   **Attendance:** 2,211.

Scorers: CITY, Walker 65.

TABLE AFTER APRIL 17TH

1.	Fleetwood (CHAMPIONS) 44	31	10	3	102-44	103
2:	Wrexham 43	28	8	7	79-30	92
3.	Mansfield 44	23	14	7	82-48	83
4.	YORK CITY 44	21	14	9	79-45	77
5.	Kidderminster................. 44	22	10	12	82-59	76
6.	Luton Town.................... 43	20	14	9	75-42	74
7.	Southport....................... 44	20	12	12	68-66	72

NOW FOR Braintree. No matter that City had walloped the Essex men 6-2 in October. A win would put the Minstermen on 80 points, and in the play-offs no matter what happened in the Luton v Kidderminster game. A draw would put City one more win from play-off certainty. It looked like 80 points would get us there, so all the City faithful begged for 80 points by 5 O'clock.

Parslow came in for the injured Doig, and Fyfield for Oyebanjo. Musselwhite remained in goal, as Michael Ingham was taking no chances on his sore shin.

City's legendary striker Arthur Bottom had sadly passed away earlier in the week. City certainly needed a striker of half his calibre to shoot them into play-off Heaven this fine afternoon.

Early on, City's patient, passing game came to the fore, as Braintree seemed to prefer the more direct approach. It was a clash of styles in the early stages. The unlucky Chambers had a header against the post on the quarter-hour mark, and then Musselwhite had to be alert to keep out a rising shot from Billy Gibson.

There was huge consternation on City faces just before the half-hour mark. A mistake from Smith allowed Sean Marks a run on goal, and the striker seemed to have been brought down by Musselwhite's despairing dive to stop him going on to score. After a horrible few seconds the City fans were waiting nervously to see what would happen next. City had no other keeper on the bench.

Mercifully, it was Marks who was penalised, for simulation. After having received a yellow earlier, he was on his way to the bath, and City had a man advantage. Phew!

Astonishingly, that man Jason Walker, with 18 goals behind him, some of them downright spectacular, missed an open goal from fully three yards out. Inexplicably he crashed his shot against the bar, and then the follow-up shot by McLaughlin hit the bar again, then Chambers had his shot saved by Nathan McDonald. It was all going on at the Amlin Stadium. No score at the break.

Now it was a ding-dong battle in the second half. The ten men had their chances, and so did City. Potts lifted a shot over the bar, and Chambers had yet another shot easily saved. He hadn't scored since Darlington, in darkest January. Next up, Challinor, Walker (again), and Meredith all missed chances, but still that priceless goal would not arrive for City.

Erik Tonne came on for McLaughlin on 71 minutes. Just moments later, the Sheffield United loanee put City into Dreamland with their most glorious moment of the season yet. Chambers fed Walker, who sent the Norwegian through on goal. From 12 yards out he sent the City fans into raptures as he slid home City's goal. He became the 19th player to score for the Minstermen this season. None of the others had been half as vital as that one.

City held on fairly comfortably for their 6th win out of the last 7 on the road, and they had created a record for only losing three away games all season. What's more they now had 80 points, AND THEY KNEW THEY WERE IN THE PLAY-OFFS. Glory be.

The cat would eat well tonight, and so would I. Fish and Chips all round.

At Kenilworth Road, Luton beat Kidderminster 1-0, and were looking good themselves. But City were there, and they were jubilant. No matter what happened in their final game, their season was still on course, and everyone connected with York City was in party mood. There was still work yet to do, in May. Only half the job was done.

BRAINTREE: McDonald, Paine, Wells, Bailey-Dennis, Peters (Quinton), Gibson, (Guy), Davis, O'Connor, Reason (Simons), Marks, Wright.

YORK CITY: Musselwhite, Challinor, Fyfield, Potts, Smith, Parslow, Meredith, McLaughlin (Tonne 71) Walker (Ashikodi 90), Chambers (Brown 82), Blair.

Subs not used: Reed, Blinkhorn.

BRAINTREE 0   CITY 1   Attendance: 1,129.

Scorer: CITY, Tonne.

THE GLORIOUS TABLE SATURDAY APRIL 21ST

1.	Fleetwood T 45	31	10	4	102-46	103
2.	Wrexham 44	28	8	8	79-32	92
3.	Mansfield 45	24	14	7	84-48	86
4.	YORK CITY 45	22	14	9	80-45	80
5.	Luton Town 44	21	14	9	76-42	77
6.	Kidderminster 45	22	10	13	82-60	76
7.	Southport 45	20	13	12	71-69	73

On Tuesday night, Luton drew at Gateshead, and were 2 points behind City. The Minstermen had a goal-difference of plus 35, and the Hatters was plus 34. Even if City drew their final game a 2-goal win for Luton would put the Hatters into 4th place. Wrexham or Mansfield awaited.

CITY'S players and supporters could actually enjoy their final game of the Blue Square Premier, knowing that their play-off place was in the bag. It only remained to see whether they could finish 4th or 5th in the final sequence.

The visitors, Forest Green had had a brilliant season by their standards, and they were in 8th spot, only 7 points behind Luton. They would probably be a threat next season if they continued to improve again, especially with some heavy amounts of cash at their disposal (so the non-league grapevine said).

City's side was unrecognisable from the usual line-up. Only five who started at Braintree were included in the starting line-up. Musselwhite, after 2 remarkable clean sheets was trying for his 3rd shut-out in a row. Challinor, Fyfield, Parslow and Potts were the others who retained their places.

In came Scott Brown, Chris Doig, Erik Tonne, Matthew Blinkhorn, Moses Ashikodi, and Adriano Moke. It was virtually a City reserve side but nobody cared a jot. The point was that City's major "stars" were rested for the rigours of the play-offs starting in just four days time. We all hoped and prayed that Michael Ingham would return for them.

So, the game itself was a pedestrian affair, unsurprisingly so. Rovers had nothing to lose. Their time would come next season, but hopefully not against the City men. Youngsters Jamie Turley and Eddie Oshodi at the back contained the new-fangled City attack of Tonne, Ashikodi and Blinkhorn, whilst veteran Musselwhite seemed to watch engrossed as the ball went on to hit his post, and he held on to his record of not conceding a single goal in his mini-spell between the sticks.

For City, Brown had the only chance of a quiet first half, as he forced keeper Russell into a save.

In the second half, Reed and Pilkington came on for a little run-around but there was no real urgency required now. It would have been nice for City to produce a rare home win at the end, in case Luton managed to put 2 past Fleetwood.

City must have heard that Luton were achieving just exactly that, and after 70 minutes they were actually ahead of City in the table, as they were 2-up at Highbury.

Adriano Moke changed all that. Ten minutes from time he hit a hopeful shot which squirmed under the hands of keeper Sam Russell, and City were ahead. It was a long awaited goal at home, and a long awaited first home victory in 6 attempts. City had done all their hard work on their travels, winning 6 out of their last 7, and that's what earned them their play-off place. It finished 1-0 to the City.

That goal was important to put City in 4th, ahead of Luton. They duly won 2-0 at Fleetwood, who were probably, hung over from their own promotion celebrations.

Regular season over. It would be Mansfield Town at home on Wednesday night. Then the hard work would begin in earnest.

Shortly after the final whistle it was celebration time for City's fans and players. Gary Mills dragged his entire squad around the ground, including poor Scotty Kerr, whose season ended in March.

We're in the play-offs, players do a well deserved lap of honour.
(Picture The Press, York).

I can honestly say it was then that it really struck me what an awesome squad of players we had at our club. Practically every one of the 25 players who remained, plus youngsters Reece Kelly, and Ben White had all played a significant part in our success. (They will all be detailed in a separate Chapter).

Just look at all the talent City had, and they all were waving triumphantly as they did their lap of honour around the Crescent.

Keepers Ingham and Musselwhite (three clean sheets, out of three), A plethora of defenders had all played their part; Challinor, Oyebanjo, Fyfield, Smith, McGurk, together with newcomers Doig and Gibson.

Then the midfield artisans, Kerr and McLaughlin, Potts, and Brown, and Bopp, and the inimitable Matty Blair, and Pilkington and Moke, and James Meredith who figured in midfield and at full-back. Danny Parslow had also been a defender-turned-midfielder in recent weeks.

And then the glory-boys, the strikers. Jason Walker, 18 goals and wonder goal in October, Jamie Reed our super-sub, Ashley Chambers, Matthew Blinkhorn, Moses Ashikodi, and last but not least, Erik Tonne whose goal actually clinched a play-off spot.

We saluted them all as they passed the Shippo-end. They had been magnificent, every one of them, and we were so, so proud.

Poor Scotty Kerr was given his reward for hobbling round the pitch, he looked in agony, poor chap. He was presented with the prestigious Player of the Season Award. The poor chap had to hobble back and forth a few more times to collect some more honours as well. He fully deserved all those accolades.

Finally, that brilliant manager Gary Mills addressed the supporters. Our job is not yet done, he said. We have to get out of this ****** League now.

He was right. The REAL job would begin on Wednesday night.

YORK CITY: Musselwhite, Challinor, Fyfield, Brown, Doig, Parslow, Tonne (Kelly 77), Potts, Blinkhorn (Pilkington 57), Ashikodi (Reed 57), Moke.

Subs not used: McLaughlin, White.

FOREST GREEN: Russell, Hodgkiss, Turley, Oshodi, Stokes, Collins, Forbes, Klukowski, Uwezu (Rowe), Taylor (Styche), Norwood.

BRAINTREE 0   CITY 1   **Attendance:** 1,129.

Scorer: CITY, Moke 82.

NB: The Final Conference table appears on page 203.

CHAPTER 12
INTO THE PLAY-OFFS

NOW FOR the play-offs. Wednesday, May the 2nd, and CITY were hosting Mansfield Town in the first leg.

For any football person, spectators or players alike play-offs are something special in the lives of all of us. Exciting, yes, nervy, yes, but this was the night we had all been hoping for since August. True, it would be wonderful to be promoted as Champions, but the play-offs provide so much drama. Such anticipation, such hope, its where all football fans hopes and dreams can live or die.

We as supporters of York City had seen it all before. Bury, 1993, Stockport County, 1994, Morecambe, 2007, and Luton, 2010. The fact was that in all four of those play-off semi-finals City had not conceded a single goal to date at Fortress Bootham.

To lose in the play-offs is deplorable, abysmal, heartbreaking, anguish. There is nothing worse than being so close to the ultimate prize, and losing at the final hurdle.

There is nothing better than to win the things . To win the semi-finals is one big step, but that is only half the story. Wembley was waiting for the winners, and we hoped it would be us.

I love the noise, the big crowd, the atmosphere, the pride, and all the flag-waving euphoria among the City faithful. It was all there on that Wednesday night. We were up for it. Here we go again.

Michael Ingham was fit for the fray, having cleared up his shin injury. Smith and Doig were the preferred centre-back pairing after all the chopping and changing we had seen this season. Goodness knows how many different combinations we had seen in that department. The preferred full backs were Challinor and Fyfield.

The engine room consisted of Danny Parslow, presumably as Anchor Man in Kerr's absence, Meredith, McLaughlin, and the inimitable Matty Blair out wide. Jason Walker and Ashley Chambers up front.

We were up for it; we were buzzing, but we were well aware of Mansfield's strengths. Up front was Matt Green, who terminally damaged our play-off hopes in 2010 when he scored Oxford's opener at Wembley. At the back they had a colossus, name of Exodus Geohaghon, who had been around the non-league circuit quite a while. Not only was he a supremely effective defender at this level, but he was also capable of launching deadly missiles into the box with his long throws. Mansfield were well-known for their "no-nonsense" attitude, if that's the correct phrase to use. They would not be taking any prisoners that's for sure. It was going to be one heck of a battle.

Just over 6,000 of us were there. Hoping for a positive result. Hoping for something special. The giant red and blue flags were raised as the players entered the arena, and the atmosphere was electric.

City roared into action straight away, as they attacked the Shippo End in the first half (normally just the opposite of what they would prefer to do). City gained an immediate corner, taken by McLaughlin, who launched it into the box and Chris Doig headed over the bar, after a poor clearance by Mansfield.

Every time Mansfield had a throw in, that giant, Geohaghon came running up to take them. The first of his "missiles" was headed wide, to the relief of the City defence, by Anthony Howell. The danger signs were there.

On another Mansfield raid, Howell headed over the bar from a cross by Gary Roberts, and City breathed again.

On City's next attack, euphoria from City fans, but short-lived, sadly. Matty Blair stuck the ball in the net after Smith's original shot came to him. So near, but yet so far. The goal was ruled out for offside.

A dangerous free-kick from Luke O'Neill, thankfully went sailing over the bar into the Mansfield throngs. There were 1,352 visiting supporters, apparently.

On 26 minutes, Geohaghon launched an "Exocet" deep into the City area. Matty Blair and Ross Dyer went up for the ball, and Dyer got there first. The ball was in the net in an instant and City had been undone by the one thing they had feared. Set-pieces, in particular long throws. They had already had their first warning, but this one cost them their first goal ever conceded in a play-off semi-final at the Crescent, and it hurt. Well, it certainly hurt me, anyway.

City had to come back straight away. I don't know why, perhaps its the pessimist in me, but I always truly believe that City find it harder to score at the "Away" End of the ground. I may be wrong, but maybe History will prove my point.

City had the "advantage" of playing to the Shippo, and HAD to take advantage of that before the break. Ashley Chambers had a 15-yard shot easily saved by Alan Marriott. Come on City, let's have one before half-time. Please.

In the 42nd minute, Jon Challinor went racing down the right wing, and he delivered a delicious-looking cross across the box with any number of players waiting in the middle. The first player it hit was that man Exodus Geohaghon, and he sliced it past his own keeper into the net. Our prayers were answered, and we were jumping up and down like lunatics.

City had them on the run. Jason Walker had an ambitious effort from over 30 yards, which had Marriott scrambling back to save. Walker then dragged another shot across goal after a header on from Chambers. City fans were baying for another, and it was wonderful to be back in play-off action after 2 years. We wanted another by half-time, but it would not come. The noise became ever louder.

In fact the visitors finished the half on top. Ingham had to charge off his line to head clear, as the ever-dangerous Green came rushing at him. The Mansfield striker actually seemed to clatter into Ingham, and was duly cautioned for his rash challenge. Next, Lindon Meikle fired over a vicious drive from 15 yards, and that was half-time. 1-1 and all to play for. We were a quarter of the way through the tie.

The second half was just as frenzied, atmosphere-wise, at least. Matty Blair was again off target with a disappointing effort, and then Green lifted a good chance over, after Dyer had stormed past Jamal Fyfield as though he was invisible. Whoops.

Poor Jamal was having a "Mare" for a few minutes now. Next, he dangled his leg as Gary Roberts beat him, and could have easily been dismissed if he made contact; he had already been booked in the first half. Howell's shot hit Ingham in the chest, and City survived.

Adam Murray sent a searching through ball into the path of Green on 74 minutes. In chasing the ball, the dangerous hit-man's momentum carried him into a collision course with Ingham, and the striker seemed to handle the ball. The referee brandished a yellow card, and that was that.

Green, having been booked for a dangerous challenge in the first half was a goner. Advantage City now, for sure. I could fully understand how Mansfield felt about the harshness of it all, I really could. Had it been a Walker or a Blair or a Chambers it had happened to, I would have felt the same way too.

City had to press home the advantage now. We were all discussing the prospect of Matt Green missing the second leg, as that would surely be the case now.

Smithy headed over a great chance from Meredith's cross, and Jon Challinor fired wide from 25 yards. Matty Blair drove over from the edge of the box, and then Moke, who had replaced Paddy McLaughlin, headed over a cross from Challinor.

City's winner on the night failed to materialise. Moke had a final, almost desperate, long-shot deep into injury time but Marriott saved it comfortably.

All to play for now.

YORK CITY: Ingham, Challinor, Fyfield, Parslow, Smith, Doig, Meredith, McLaughlin, (Moke 82), Walker, Chambers, Blair.

Subs not used: Musselwhite, Reed, Potts, Brown.

MANSFIELD TOWN: Marriott, O'Neill, Riley (Andrew), Geohaghon, Sutton, Murray, Roberts, Howell, Dyer (Rhead) Green, Meikle (Briscoe).

CITY 1   MANSFIELD 1   Attendance: 6,057.

Scorers: CITY, Geohaghon (og) 42   **MANSFIELD,** Dyer 26.

Mansfield's fans were singing. They were happy with the draw. City were not especially unhappy, after only losing 3 away games all season. We had just won 6 of our last 7 league games on the road, and had not conceded a single away goal in our last 3 games.

Mansfield's Exodus Geohaghon puts through his own net to put City
on level terms.

(Picture The Press, York).

Off to Field Mill next Monday. Unfortunately I would be working until 1 O'clock.

C'est la vie

The time passed quickly before Monday came around. There had been some kind of a disturbance involving the partner of Mansfield's Chairman after the first leg, but that has been well chronicled elsewhere. I will not go into it.

Ted was there, amongst the City faithful turn-out of nearly 1,500. My chum Graham had subscribed to "PREMIER SPORTS" TV so he kindly invited me over to his place to watch the game with him.

Arriving home at around 1.35 my stupid car decided not to work. I ask you, what a time to have a flat battery. I was on my bike, quite literally, and sped off like that Cavendish bloke from the Isle of Man who always seems to wear a green jersey. I was off like the clappers as I didn't want to miss a single second of the game.

CITY had dropped Jamal Fyfield, in favour of Lanre Oyebanjo, who would play in midfield; James Meredith would take the left-back slot.

I arrived at Graham's, sweating like an over-fed Mongolian Pig about to be chucked on to the hog-roast, just in time to see the first missile launched by Exodus Geohaghon after 4 minutes. (I do not know what happened before that, nothing much, I gather).

City dealt with that one fairly comfortably, as they would be destined to do all day.

Once I settled down after my ridiculous 2-mile cycling dash, I watched a cagey, kind of cat-and-mouse first period. City really only had one decent chance; it came from Paddy McLaughlin who missed the target. In actual fact he had another chance from long range which also failed to test Marriott, and that was that.

Naturally, Mansfield had their chances too. A shot by Adam Murray was blocked magnificently by Danny Parslow, who diverted it safely over the bar, after Michael Ingham had failed to react to a back-header to him from Jon Challinor.

Lindon Meikle, the Stags lively and highly-rated winger was causing problems, and he forced Ingham into a save after one of his liveliest breaks.

Half-time came and it was still a stalemate. No goals during the past 90 minutes of the tie, since half-time in the first leg. It was one of those games where it seemed that one goal would settle it. We hoped and prayed that it would be the Minstermen who would do just that.

Not for the first time this season, City stepped up the pace in the second half. A shot by Jason Walker was blocked by Gary Roberts after Marriott had dropped a header from Chris Smith.

We're on our way to Wembley (Twice).
(Picture The Press, York).

Next, Matty Blair cut in from the right to force Marriott into making a decent save. A few minutes later the 17-goal winger had an ambitious shot from 30 yards when he could have probably taken it further and try to beat the keeper from close range.

Mansfield came back into it. They were undefeated at home in 13 games, and they were never going to lie down quietly, even without their missing striker Matt Green. On the hour mark, Louis Briscoe unleashed a dangerous drive which warmed Ingham's hands, and then, substitute Moke kicked a wickedly swerving corner off the line, but the referee had already blown up for a foul on Ingham anyway.

Meikle fired into the side-netting from the edge of the box, and then City came back into their own.

Another substitute, young Michael Potts (who had replaced McLaughlin) released Blair down the right, and his cross was stepped over by Walker, only for Moke to shoot wildly over from 15 yards when he had an excellent chance to put City into Dream-land.

Mansfield were looking ever-dangerous now, and we were worried, very worried. Briscoe volleyed across the City goal, and then Murray fired over from 20 yards after Meredith had headed a Geohaghon long throw straight to him.

After a nervy last few minutes as far as City fans were concerned, City battled on. Substitute Matt Rhead, another giant for the Stags, also had a dangerous attempt, but Smith had blocked it and the Minstermen hung on. Their work was far from done. Tired legs or not.

Stamina would be ever important now for both sides, as we entered dreaded extra-time. City seemed to be getting stronger to my way of thinking.

Michael Potts, had not had much chance to shine in McLaughlin's shadow this season. Midway through the first half of extra-time, he jinked his way into the Mansfield box, and saw his shot go sadly wide.

Next, a Meikle shot was comfortably saved by Ingham, and Moke's shot was held by Marriott, after good work from Ashley Chambers.

Oh my goodness. Just fifteen minutes left and the dreaded "P" word was entering our thoughts. We did not wish for that.

Stag's sub, Lee Stevenson got into a dangerous position, but failed to bother Ingham, as his shot was weak and easily saved.

The dreaded Penalties were nine minutes away from happening. Jamal Fyfield, who had just replaced Chris Doig at the end of normal time, released Jason Walker for a run down the left. He pretended to shimmy past defender Murray, but instead chipped an inch-perfect cross straight into open space where Matty Blair came steaming in to plant it in the net, in spite of challenges from the Mansfield backs, and it was glorious.

I jumped out of my chair, and Graham did the same. We were there, with all those fifteen-hundred City faithful at Field Mill. We were there with them in spirit, and we could see them jumping up and down behind the goal where Matty scored. Ted was there, somewhere, lucky lucky Ted, et, all.

Goodness knows I could not bear to watch. It was so near, but so far away, still yet.

Seconds after City's glorious goal, left back Ritchie Sutton received his second yellow card for a trip on Matty Blair, and he was gone for his early bath. Things were favouring City once again.

All they had to do was survive for ten more minutes. Another Geohaghon missile hurtled towards Ingham's goal, and but for his vital save it would have been a carbon copy of Dyer's first leg goal by that same player, but gladly the City keeper held on this time.

The best thing was that City kept on going for the second, and that was the only option now. To back-pedal would be to favour the Stags, but City took the game to them instead. Good job (for my nerves at any rate).

City were almost rampant now, with Wembley in their sights (again). Walker missed an excellent chance, he tried to chip the keeper, but luckily for Mansfield, Luke O'Neill cleared off the line.

Our Jason could have had a hat-trick. For some strange reason he messed about so long before delivering an apology of a shot which Marriott smothered, then the follow-up attempt by Walker was easily saved as well. What a waste it was but we hoped it would not matter.

Four minutes injury time said the 4th official. That was four minutes too long for me. Then jubilation. It was over, and WE WERE THERE.

Graham got a hug from me. Who cares. Bring it on. Let's go to Wembley twice. Course we can afford it. Of that there was no doubt. Wembley twice inside eight days. This must be Dream-land now .

MANSFIELD TOWN: Marriott, O'Neill, Riley, Geohaghon, Sutton, Roberts, Murray, Howell (Rhead), Briscoe (Stevenson), Dyer, Meikle.

YORK CITY: Ingham, Challinor (Moke 61), Meredith, Parslow, Smith, Doig (Fyfield 87) Oyebanjo, McLaughlin (Potts 72), Walker, Chambers, Blair.

Subs not used: Musselwhite, Read.

MANSFIELD 0   CITY 1   **Aggregate: 2-1 CITY**   **Attendance:** 7,295.

Scorer: CITY, Blair 111.

I needed some fresh air. I needed to run around somewhere, and shout it loud, and proud.

"CITY ARE OFF TO WEMBLEY . . . . TWICE"

Graham's girlfriend kindly made me a massive bowl of pasta. I hardly did it justice as my nerves were not recovered yet.

We watched the first half of the Wrexham-Luton second leg. Luton had won the first leg 2-0, and went ahead with a penalty at the Racecourse to lead by 3 on aggregate. I gave up, and headed home after Graham had persuaded me to down a can of lager. It was celebration time for us, but things were happening in North Wales.

Wrexham pulled two back, but sadly went down 3-2 to the Hatters, on aggregate.

Oh no, not them again.

Some pal of mine told me he would not go to Wembley if THEY were playing against us. I will not name him.

Oh well, let's go to Wembley twice. Here we go then chaps.

CHAPTER 13

WEMBLEY III: THE FA TROPHY FINAL

SOME PEOPLE were callously calling this the "Dress Rehearsal" for the big one under the Arch next Sunday. So be it.

Nobody likes to lose at Wembley, whether it's the final of the Johnstone's Paint Trophy, the Carling Cup Final, or especially the play-off Finals, really. It is not a pretty place to be on any such occasion.

City had already been there and lost the Trophy Final in 2009, to Stevenage, a better side at the time. In this glorious season of 2011-12, City had escaped from being dumped out of the Competition at the very first hurdle; but for Jon Challinor's dubious equaliser against Solihull in the dying seconds, the Minstermen would not have passed square one.

No, joking apart, you always need to win at Wembley, and you always want to. Of course you do.

City had failed to beat Newport County twice, in the space of 2 weeks just last month, despite the difference of 15 positions in the final league standings. County had beaten City at their place when they were desperate for points to stay in the Conference, and inflicted City's first defeat in 14 away games then. In the return at Bootham Crescent they would have taken all the points but for Jason Walker's timely return to something like full fitness once again. They were no mugs.

Peter Moss and John Uttley were the organisers of the "Harrogate Minstermen" supporters club. They were good lads and they always did a sterling job taking City fans all over this nation of ours.

But, for goodness sake, lads, half-past five in the morning, what unearthly time of day is that, I ask you ??

Yes, the coach was leaving Boroughbridge at 5.30, so I had to be up and running before the break of dawn at 4.15 to get myself moving, and ready for my 25-minute walk to town. The birds were singing, and so was I (but not out loud, you understand).

A few lads I knew from the town were there, who wouldn't often be seen at the Crescent, but what the heck, it was great to know that City would be backed by nearly 10,000 on the day, and that was all that mattered. The hours passed quickly, once we had taken all our passengers on board from Knaresborough, Harrogate, Wetherby and Garforth, and everybody was in good spirits.

We found ourselves at Bushey, Hertfordshire, at 10.45. This had been chosen by John and Peter as a handy place for a refreshment stop ever since we got to new Wembley for the first time in 2009. It hadn't been so lucky for us yet, but we hoped our luck would change, this time.

We had 2¼ hours to kill. Rather than to spend all our time waiting for the pub to open, we went for a little walk (my chum Dave and I).

One of us, I can't remember who it was, decided that we should walk to the outskirts of Watford, just down the road, and so we did that, in the end, that is. We had to ask a police-woman which way Watford was, as one of us had decided to walk in completely the wrong direction in the first place.

"I told you it was the other way, you muppet", Dave said to me. "I saw some buses going the other way with WATFORD on the front."

It was a beautiful morning in early Summer (or late spring to be precise). I saw a single magpie in a bush, and refused to take another step further till I saw its mate. (That's some kind of superstitious stuff I knew).

Dave thought I was being a bit of an idiot. He probably was right. Further down the road there was a chap walking with his dog. I stopped to ask him if we were far from Watford's football ground, and we started talking about Yorkshire a lot as he had visited our glorious County many times. He wished City well for the final.

Meanwhile, Dave had spotted a field with some Shetland ponies in it. I was off to catch up with him and found him suddenly engaged in conversation with a pretty lass who had just dropped by to feed some of those ponies, and they were chatting away as if they were lifelong friends. Ah well.

We took a liking to this pretty little suburb, just outside London, really.

We returned to Bushey High street around 12.15 and ate our nosh, or some of it. Back in the Red Lion the City fans were having a relaxing couple of hours before the short half-hour trip to the Stadium. This was how we liked it, and this was the way, it would always be, for every Wembley Trip. I understand the landlord and his wife had "emigrated" from Liverpool many years ago, and settled in this little Hertfordshire Town. We would be back in 8 days time.

Our coach drew up at the Stadium at 1.50 as we passed all the "anoraks" marking coach numbers in their little books. Crikey, I thought that I was an anorak with my football stats, but that must be even worse than me, surely.

We had to find Ted. He would no doubt have plenty of things to do, and plenty of people to talk to. He knew practically every single person who supported City anyway. He would probably be standing up above the steps at the York End of the Stadium watching for people he knew on their way up to the turnstiles.

And he was. We found him at 2 O'clock, and we all talked and mingled for a while as kick-off time approached. Personally I wasn't all that nervous. You could bet your last pound I would be next Sunday though.

We managed to drag ourselves into the Stadium just after half past two. It was good to be back at our National Stadium for our third visit in 4 years, we were well familiar with the place by now. Newport probably had 11,000 supporters to City's 9,000 or so. I think I am right to say it was their first visit to the New Wembley, so it was a great experience for them.

We were perched high up this time, underneath the balcony roof, adjacent to the press and presentation area, not far from the half-way line. There was talk of maybe resting a couple of key players for City's far bigger match next Sunday, but Gary Mills was having none of that.

The only change from the side which got us to the play-off Final was that Ben Gibson came in at left-back, and Doig was out. Danny Parslow would revert to centre-back alongside skipper Smith. This was the 100th match being staged at New Wembley, and City's first goal would be their 100th of this remarkable season, all told.

For most of City's players, in fact, all of them apart from Ingham and Meredith, it was their first time on the Hallowed turf, but I understand that Challinor had played for Cambridge there. It was therefore a nervy start, which Newport seemed to handle better than the City players, really. (Parslow was on the bench in 2010).

Apart from an early corner by City, after Blair's deflected shot, the result of which Smith headed into the Newport keeper's hands, it was the men from Wales who were on top.

Young striker Romone Rose had a dangerous attempt pushed away by Michael Ingham, after he had skipped past Challinor. Then the ex-QPR youngster, alarmingly for us, found himself on a clear run on goal in the 9th minute, after Nat Jarvis had sent him through. Sadly for Newport, his weak effort went straight into Michael Ingham's hands, and the City fans behind the goal, and elsewhere, breathed a huge sigh of relief.

Newport continued to show City the way; they had remained unbeaten by the Minstermen in the league, and they were not short of confidence in the early stages. Romone Rose again threatened. He then had a long range shot deflected wide by Chris Smith, before a deep cross from David Pipe was headed wide by Ismail Yakubu.

City came into the game at last. Paddy McLaughlin, who had scored 13 goals this season, launched a shot from 25 yards which spun off County's skipper Gary Warren, and was deflected wide, and Matty Blair had another attempt which was headed away to safety by Newport.

Rose and Jarvis missed a chance apiece, and then City ended the half on top as the Welsh lads tired.

A dangerous free-kick by McLaughlin went just wide, and then James Meredith dragged a volley wide from the edge of the box, before Jon Challinor had a stinging long-range shot, saved.

Newport had the final chance of the half, as Lee Minshull beat Smithy to a challenge but put his shot wide.

City are a second half team, which the records clearly showed this season. They were still waiting for their 100th goal in all competitions; surely it would soon be coming.

Lanre Oyebanjo had an ambitious long-range effort which failed to find the target, then County's Sam Foley had a shot off target, moments later.

It was the 65th minute on the Wembley Stadium clock. Ashley Chambers, near the half-way line, launched a hopeful through ball looking to pick out Matty Blair. Keeper Glyn Thompson was rushing out to meet the speedy City winger, who decided in a flash to lob the ball over him. It seemed like time was frozen still. We gawped in wonderment as the ball went sailing slowly, agonizingly on towards the net. It seemed like everything was in slow motion, and we were on our feet in jubilation as the net was finally bulging. Pandemonium ensued. It was a brilliant opportunist goal and it was our 100th of the season, and it was our first proper goal at New Wembley, and we were in front at last (our goal in 2010 was an own goal scored by an Oxford player). Glory be. It was a wonderful moment in what had been a wonderful season up till now.

That was Matty's 8th goal in the FA Trophy; and strangely enough, Jason Walker hadn't scored a single one. No matter, City were getting stronger now, as Newport's spirits seemed to sag at last.

Romone Rose continued his unfortunate afternoon with another shot that missed the target from some way out.

The Minstermen showed their superiority next in a dazzling move so typical of their early season form. A delicious through ball from McLaughlin sent Chambers surging down the right. He had registered the most assists for City this season, and he whipped a cross into the centre to find Lanre Oyebanjo come storming in to sweep the ball into the net from three yards out. It was a lightning raid, and it delighted all the City following. It was a peach of a goal in the way it was fashioned, and it brought a lot of smiles to a lot of faces, mine included. I was as happy as a sand-boy in a pit of sand with a lot of sand.

Wembley belonged to us at last. We had conquered it. Poor Newport. Their players heads dropped after that. They were beaten, and they were out for the count. You had to feel for them. We had seen it all before.

Not much happened after that. There were late attempts from Foley, Warren and Yakubu, but they failed to bother Michael Ingham really, although Yakubu's effort actually hit the foot of the post. In stoppage time, Jason Walker had a spectacular volley which went high and wide.

But the cup was ours, and the glorious celebrations could now begin.

This was City's first ever Trophy in a National competition. Smithy raised the Cup on high. Photographers both amateur and Professional alike were snapping away like there was no tomorrow.

I, myself was in the aisles to get a better view of the celebrations, leaving poor Dave transfixed in his seat, as I went to snap the players celebrating.

The City players were amassed, with the Trophy, smiling and waving to the fans. Michael Ingham "dived" across the winners board as though he was saving a penalty or something, and then they made their (half) lap of honour in front of the jubilant supporters. This was some Party, but there would be a heck of a bigger one next Sunday, if we happened to be successful. That was just another dream right now.

Everyone was happy. I drifted out of the stadium with Ted not far behind me. In the aftermath of victory I was busy taking photos of all the celebrations, and Dave was left behind.

Outside the Stadium there were handshakes from City supporters after the game. Sean was there, from Boroughbridge, and, apparently Graham had caught up with Dave, and ambushed him before giving him a gigantic hug. Graham's girlfriend was waving from on top of the steps, and I had vanished off in front towards our coach.

The Newport, fans, the few of whom remained, were gracious and most dignified at their defeat. A few of them came over to returning City fans, and wished us well for the Promotion play-offs. It was heart-warming to see such gracious supporters like that. Newport had enjoyed their day out, and they, like City in 2009 had done themselves proud by getting to the Final. They were also staying up, and they were well happy with their season.

For City, on the other hand, there were far more important things to sort out yet. Yes, we would enjoy our Trophy victory all the way back to York, but next Sunday was always on our minds.

It was a happy journey home.

YORK CITY: Ingham, Challinor, Gibson, Oyebanjo, Smith, Parslow, Meredith, McLaughlin (Fyfield 83), Walker (Reed 90), Chambers (Moke 90), Blair.

Captain Chris Smith proudly holds the FA Trophy aloft.
(Picture The Press, York).

NEWPORT COUNTY: Thompson, Pipe, Warren, Yakubu, Hughes, Porter (Knights), Evans, Foley, Jarvis (Harris), Minshull, Rose (Buchanan).

CITY 2   NEWPORT 0   Attendance: 19,844.

Scorers: CITY, Blair 65; Oyebanjo. 72.

On the following Thursday, May the 17th, after 9 long hours of talks, it was finally announced that planning permission had been given to York City to build a new stadium at Monks Cross, on the outskirts of the City.

This had been a tremendous boost to the club, and manager Gary Mills in this, the single most important week in the History of our glorious football team.

This was the icing on the cake. Had City not been granted permission to go ahead on the scheme, the very future of York City would have been in severe danger, to say the least.

This was the second part of Gary Mills' dreams coming true this season. Wembley awaited for part three of that noble dream.

CHAPTER 14

WEMBLEY IV: THE PLAY-OFF FINAL

SUNDAY May the 20th, 2012 had arrived. This was the big one. Our wonderful season ended right here. It was our day of destiny; it would either be glory, or absolute misery, nothing in between.

Everything would be fine. According to my mate, Graham (Brad) Bradley, we had nothing to worry about. He told me in early April that City would get to Wembley twice, and that we would win both times. We had already beaten Newport in the Trophy Final. I thought about Brad's words many times that day. He had also forecasted that we would beat Luton 2-1 in the play-off Final.

Nobody could guarantee that. Luton had only beaten City once, in 10 clashes since the Hatters came down to the Conference. There was a nasty feeling in my mind that it was their turn to win this time, and this one mattered the most by far.

Peter and John had us leaving Boroughbridge at 5.30 once again. There was talk of leaving an hour later this time but it didn't happen. Bleary-eyed, I left home at the unearthly hour of 5 am, and met up with Dave at the end of Roecliffe Lane. Here we go again.

We stopped at Leicester Forest around 9. Luckily for us, our coach was the first to arrive, otherwise we would have faced a stampede to get into the loo with all the rest of the City fans. I was watching out for Ted arriving on the Travel Club coach, as the convoy of 20 buses arrived. I stood in the corridor and gawped in wonderment as 1,000 red and blue clad City fans filed past in just a few minutes. The usual suspects were there, Fletch and Trigger, Phil, Steve Atkinson, and William, Peter Moss's nephew. I talked to him a while. No sign of Ted.

The little Hertfordshire town of Bushey, and all its delights, awaited us once again. It was my third stop there, and I knew the way to Watford by now. Graham, Dave, and I went on the same walk which Dave and I enjoyed just eight days earlier. We went to see the ponies again, but didn't speak to any of the locals on this occasion.

Just for luck, we walked on to the outskirts of Watford, and we turned round at the exact same spot as we had done last Saturday, before returning to Bushey High Street to eat our lunch.

Huddersfield Town were playing at MK Dons in their League One play-off first leg tie. We watched the first few minutes on telly at our 'local', the Red Lion, before returning to our coach at 1 O'Clock.

Once we spotted the famous arch from a couple of miles away, the nerves, for me, at least, started kicking in. Goodness knows how the players were feeling.

We got to Wembley at 1.45. This was our second home by now. It was City's fourth visit in as many seasons. It was agreed that we would meet Ted at the Bobby Moore statue once again, and we found him without any trouble. Graham went off to meet his folks, and join the City fans behind the goal. Our seats were on the Northern touchline.

I had a job to do. I had to buy some Wembley souvenirs for my brother Neil, and his son Robert, who were exiled half-way across the World in the Philippines. I felt for them both, at having to miss the best season in City's History for many years, and I thought about them all day. They had been at Wembley in 2009 and 2010, and had listened to every City game on the Internet link this season, having to get up at 4 in the morning for evening games.

There was a different atmosphere today, from the Newport game. I could sense it as I walked down the stairway at the West end of the Stadium. I should have gone back to the Eastern side where the City fans were approaching from. One person in red and blue, with 20,000 Orange-clad fans coming towards me. I hid my City scarf from view, and ran the gauntlet of the Luton fans until I reached the point where the two entrance walkways converged. Naturally I joined the Eastern walkway as soon as I could.

Wembley Way was full of colour as usual, a mass of orange and white, red, and blue, everywhere you looked. Souvenirs, many at rip-off prices were there for the taking. I ended up being festooned in two City flags and three scarves in bright blue and red, and mingled safely with the City fans at last. Luton fans outnumbered us by four or five to one, but there were plenty of City supporters to talk to. It was 2.30, and time to make my way to the stadium. I could see Ted talking to Dave, above the Eastern steps, and I waved all my flags and scarves at them. At the top of the steps, I signalled that I would meet them at the turnstiles. I had done enough walking already, thank you very much.

We entered Wembley Stadium (the New one), for the fourth time. We dearly hoped that this visit would be the best one of the lot.

Inside, the noise the Luton fans were making was terrifying to me. It was as though the 8,000 City fans had gate-crashed their party, really. I hoped that the City players would not be intimidated by all that row. They knew who they were playing for, and I knew they had their focus. They had sampled the Wembley atmosphere just eight days earlier, and had already tasted victory at the National Stadium. They had seen it all before.

In the City line-up, Chris Doig returned to join Chris Smith, from the Trophy Final, replacing Danny Parslow, who would play the anchor role in midfield with Meredith and Oyebanjo joining him in the engine room. Paddy McLaughlin, who had figured in every game but two in the League season had been left out. I felt sorry for him, and wondered what the reason for his omission was.

Luton, blasted off like a retro-rocket. In the space of 60 seconds, Robbie Willmot twice stormed down the left, and ran at Challinor. They were like a bunch of rottweilers out for the kill, and they wanted blood. They got it after 70 seconds. Willmott passed inside for Andre Gray to fire in off Ingham's post before he could blink. I swear to this day that awesome racket the Luton fans were making had given them the impetus for that first goal start. I don't know about anybody else, but they certainly frightened me.

I was in deep shock for a good while afterwards. I was speechless. Some people, cruelly had said that some 20,000 of the Luton fans were just day-trippers. No matter, they were still making one almighty noise by now. I feared that City would be routed by the hungry Hatters, seeking glorious revenge for their recent miseries at the hands of City, and what sweet revenge it would be for them as well.

It was a good job the City players were far from bothered by their early blip. To their eternal credit they just rolled up their sleeves, and got on with the job in hand. The thing is, City had a team with bundles of confidence, and they had a fantastic spirit and passion instilled in them by Gary Mills, and they never knew when they were beaten. Goodness knows, they had come back from losing situations many times during this season already. For goodness sake, they were losing at Kenilworth Road with just ten minutes to go in March, and still snatched victory then.

Slowly but surely, the Minstermen clawed their way back into the game. A corner by City in the 3rd minute was comfortably cleared by the Hatters, then a shot by Jason Walker, following a City throw, was blocked as well. Former City man, Lawless sent a harmless 30-yard shot wide, and then a similar effort by Adam Watkins was deflected safely into Ingham's grateful hands. The dangerous Andre Gray then wasted his effort, sending it high over Ingham's bar into the City fans.

City were coming back. Jason Walker went on a run down the left, his cross was met by Oyebanjo, who stabbed it wide of the post. The ex-Histon full-back/midfielder was destined to have a memorable game.

Next, City had a free-kick headed on by Smith for Challinor to volley from 15 yards. Alex Lawless deflected it for a corner. From the flag-kick, the ball was bobbing about in the area. From my seat I could see Doig flick the ball on, and it hit the hand of Hatters left-back Jake Howells, and City had a decent shout for a penalty. Nothing was given.

Jason Walker then outjumped the giant defender Jan Kovacs (who had a spell on loan at City). From a Challinor cross, Walker's header flashed towards the Luton net, and Mark Tyler, scrambling back, just managed to keep it out, and tip it over the bar.

It was all City now. Blair had a run down the right, and fed Walker, whose shot was blocked. After some more slick passing by the Minstermen, their fourth corner ensued, and George Pilkington managed to clear it safely. Paul Buckle, the Luton manager had a concerned look on his face.

The Hatters came back into it for a while. Jon Challinor stopped the dangerous Willmott in his tracks, then Oyebanjo blocked another Lawless attempt. Andre Gray had a shot deflected for a corner, which Doig cleared, then Stuart Fleetwood sent a shot high and wide of goal.

It was a pulsating match, and it was end-to-end stuff now. City fans could sense that something was about to happen. Noise levels at the East of the Stadium increased as Pilkington clattered into Jon Challinor in the 25th minute. The Luton skipper may have got part of the ball but it did not matter. The free-kick had been given. Lanre Oyebanjo delivered it to the far post, and it was half-cleared to Chris Smith who laid it off delightfully into the path of Ashley Chambers who came steaming in like an Express Train, and lashed an unstoppable 12-yard screamer into Tyler's net. It was delicious, and it was exquisite, and it was no more than City had deserved. It was Chambers' first goal since Darlington in January, and it sent the City fans into delirium. What a time to break a scoring drought it was. City were right back in the game.

But it was Luton who hit back. Howells had a shot blocked by Challinor for a corner. Ingham dashed out yards outside his six-yard box and claimed the ball with confidence. Howells then blazed another long shot wide, and then a shot by Andre Gray seemed as though it may have hit the upper arm of Jon Challinor, but nothing was given.

The unfortunate City right back (Challinor), was feeling the effects of his ankle injury sustained in that crunching Pilkington challenge, and he was substituted by Scott Brown on 36 minutes. Lanre Oyebanjo moved to right back.

There was no let up in the action, and chances kept on coming, thick and fast. Andre Gray beat Chris Doig on another dangerous run, but Ingham parried well as he shot from the angle, and Ben Gibson cleared the danger, for a corner. Ingham was in command of his box again.

Matty Blair scorched past Kovacs on the left flank, ran on, but lost control, and the chance was gone. Into injury-time, Alex Lawless thumped a shot straight into Ingham's midriff, and then in the dying seconds of the half, Stuart Fleetwood scuffed a tame shot straight into the City keeper's hands again.

It had been a pulsating first half, and both sides had created chances galore. It was a brilliant advert for Conference Football, and the game was poised on a knife-edge. Honours even, and all to play for now.

Having finally managed to get to the loo during the interval, I was hardly in my seat when the referee's whistle blew to start the second half.

Just as Luton stormed the first minute of the first half, City began the second half just as strongly. It was all a blur to me, as I settled back into my seat. A long throw by Oyebanjo on the right was headed on by Danny Parslow and Matty Blair, who was lurking at the far post, appeared from nowhere, and side-footed into Tyler's net. Before I had time to blink, the ball was sitting in the back of the onion bag, and the East end of the Stadium was a mass of celebrating red and blue supporters. It was a glorious moment, just 68 seconds into the half, and two seconds quicker than Luton's opener.

I could not believe our luck. As I always do, I looked at the referee's assistant to make sure that the goal was good. There was no raised flag, and the referee made his way back to the centre circle. Glory be. City were ahead, and no-one, especially me, could quite believe what had just happened.

Normally, when goals are scored at Wembley, the big screens at either end of the Stadium, show an instant replay seconds later. We were waiting for the replay but it never came. It later transpired that Matty Blair had put the ball in from an offside position, but the goal was given, and that was that. City fans were not complaining, but a few people clad in orange would have been, had they seen that replay.

There was still a good 45 minutes left for City to defend their precious lead. It would be a long, long half for the City faithful to endure. James Meredith headed over from 6 yards, and Ashley Chambers had a great run to the edge of the box before shooting straight at Mark Tyler.

Luton came back at City, inevitably. Osano had a dangerous run, which was blocked by City, as Fleetwood dithered with his shot, and then it was City's turn again. Matty Blair had a typical spurt down the left flank, and his cross was met by Chambers who failed to trouble Tyler.

Paul Buckle brought on winger John-Paul Kissock, who had once played on loan at Gretna, for Adam Watkins, and ex-Crawley striker Craig McAllister came on for Stuart Fleetwood up front.

Lanre Oyebanjo was a City hero in his new role at right back once again. Andre Gray had wriggled past both Doig and Gibson, before crossing towards McAllister. Somehow, and nobody knew quite how he managed it, Oyebanjo got there a fraction of a second before the ex-Crawley man, and, stretching every muscle, he prevented an almost certain goal as he got his head on the ball just in time, and nicked it off McAllister's head, for a corner. The unfortunate McAllister's forehead made contact with Oyebanjo's head, but the Luton man came off worst and had to end his brief appearance as a substitute to be replaced by Aaron O'Connor after playing less than 10 minutes himself.

From the subsequent corner, Andre Gray found himself just 3 yards out, as the ball came to him. He took a swipe at the ball and missed, and then he took another swipe, and missed again, right in front of the baying Luton fans. Things were getting very scary now, I could hardly bear to watch any more.

Now, it was all Luton, and the pressure was on City. Willmott, Gray, and O'Connor linked up in a threatening move, which resulted in a corner. The ball came to Kissock, and his shot was blocked by Doig. Ashley Chambers was replaced by Jamie Reed for City.

Ten minutes had passed since Oyebanjo's saving header, and it seemed like an hour. Next, a cross by Curtis Osano from the right was palmed by Ingham into the path of John-Paul Kissock just three yards out, and it seemed like a certain goal. Once again, Lanre Oyebanjo was alert as ever, and came storming in to block heroically as the winger was about score. For his pains, young Kissock received a bloody nose in the clash, but thank goodness Oyebanjo was there; it could so easily have been a different story. But for those two vital challenges, City could have been 3-2 down and chasing the game, they really could.

City had a brief respite as Jason Walker was fouled with eight minutes to go. The resulting kick, by Walker himself, whistled past the angle of Tyler's bar, then Luton came back strongly once again. They were surging forward with confidence, and they were once again in charge, as their fans were baying for an equaliser. For all their possession they were not hurting City all that much. The Minstermen were defending deep, and they were blocking and harassing Luton with every ounce of strength they had. It was nervy stuff, all the same, as time dragged on. City just refused to buckle under the pressure, even though their every muscle must have been hurting by now in their weary bodies. They were made of strong stuff. Surely they would not be denied their prize now. Surely not.

Time dragged on, and on. I had no fingernails left. I had one eye on the Stadium clock, and one eye on proceedings on the pitch. Every second seemed like an hour, and it seemed like weeks ago since we had scored. The tension was growing like some nasty sickness bug festering in my stomach. It was the same for all of us. Some of the City fans were strangely muted; anxious, nervous, but just a little hopeful that their wildest dreams were coming true.

Five minutes to go. Walker was replaced by Paddy McLaughlin, who got his chance at last. Willmott was caught by Ben Gibson, who was booked for his pains as the pressure built. Parslow cleared the free-kick. Andre Gray tried to feed O'Connor, but City blocked again. Then Willmott crossed for Kissock, and the majestic Oyebanjo stopped him once again. The ball came to Robbie Willmott on the edge of the box in the last second of normal time. His shot thankfully sailed over the bar.

Four minutes of added time was signalled. It would be the longest four minutes of all our lives for sure. I was dreading the thought of Luton equalising so late into the game. If they had done that, the Hatters would be firmly in the driving seat, and City heads just may have dropped. It had been devastating to lose the 2010 play-off Final, and it hurt like mad. Wembley is a deplorable and a hideous place for losing play-off Finalists, and I could not bear the thought of losing there again. My thoughts were racing as the dream was getting nearer. I could hardly believe it was so near, but it could all have been snatched away in an instant.

By now I was counting every second on my watch, just praying for the end to come. I knew I was about to explode with joy any moment. I was kicking every ball with the players, and willing City to hold out.

O'Connor went on a dangerous run at the City defence, in the first minute of added time, but his shot went wildly off target. City had a corner but Luton won it back, and booted the ball up front. With just a few seconds remaining, the ball came to Keith Keane, via Kissock, and the midfielder hurried a weak shot from 25 yards which crept apologetically past Ingham's right hand post in the 94th minute.

Finally, as the FIFTH minute of stoppage time began, a reprieve for City at last. They were able to relax a little. From a free-kick. Scott Brown launched a long ball deep into Luton's box to waste a few more seconds. Mark Tyler had the ball in his hands, and was about to launch it one more time towards the City goal.

Too late. The Final whistle blew, and it was atomic. I was in a World of my own, completely oblivious to everything and everyone around me. Vaulting over Dave, all of a sudden I was in the aisle, punching the air in delight, and performing a ridiculous victory jig of celebration. In that moment, Wembley belonged to me, (and a few thousand others naturally).

Just like the other 8,000 City fans, I was so proud of what our boys had just achieved, and the tears of happiness were flowing. We had finally made it back at last. CITY ARE BACK. Back where we belong.

In that very same instant, Gary Mills had leapt into the air like an overgrown, demented frog, and landed on the Hallowed turf, then, kneeling down he closed his eyes and raised both arms in the air in humble supplication to the Wembley Gods. It was a moment of pure magic for all of us.

Smithy had the Trophy in his hands, and he raised it to the Wembley skies, and we were going up. Jason McGill, our jubilant Chairman was hugging every player as they passed through the presentation area, and no doubt his lovely sister Sophie was also enjoying the occasion just as much.

I was especially pleased for the wonderful family McGill that we had made it back to the Football League. They had worked so hard to help the club through eight long years of Conference football. This was the reward they so richly deserved. It should never ever be forgotten that there would have been no future for York City Football club as we know it without their influx of cash when we were about to fold. They saved the club from certain doom.

(I saw Sophie's interview on local TV. She said that she hoped the players had made a lot of people proud. The answer was a resounding yes, of course. We were proud of our wonderful players, we were proud of our wonderful manager Gary Mills, and we were especially proud to have such wonderful people as Jason, Sophie, and their family at our club. We could never wish for any better people in charge of our great club).

Jubilant again . . . City are Back promotion guaranteed.
(Picture The Press, York).

Thank you one and all ! Manager Gary Mills looks to the heavens in Triumph.
(Picture The Press, York).

Meanwhile, the West End of the stadium where the Luton fans were housed was emptying fast. Hatters fans were disappearing faster than rats deserting a sinking ship. Twenty minutes after the final whistle their end was as empty as the Marie Celeste.

City's party had only just begun. The music was blaring out, "And Tonight's gonna be a Good Night", and "We are the Champions" was being sung by all. Happy Days. I wanted those moments to last forever.

The Luton fans were all gone and the 8,000 City fans had the Stadium to themselves. That was a glorious feeling. Wembley was ours, and we had conquered it. Wembley was our second home, we had been there four times in the past four seasons.

We had also conquered Luton Town our fiercest rivals, once and for all. They must have been absolutely sick and tired at the misery that City had caused them in the past three seasons.

Somehow, there had to be just a little sympathy for them, as their supporters trudged away disconsolately from the Stadium, and made their way back to their Bedfordshire homes.

We all knew how they were feeling, as we had been there ourselves. They had lost two play-off Finals running, and as for poor Alex Lawless, he had personally lost three play-offs running, having played for City in their 2010 defeat by Oxford. You can bet he was wishing he had stayed at City instead. Bad choice, Alex, mate. I hope the Wembley dressing rooms had sturdy doors.

Our Wembley party was over after half an hour, but there would be plenty more celebrations in the next 24 hours. City supporters were returning to their coaches, hugging and kissing everyone in sight, everyone they knew, and certainly everyone they did not know as well. (I was). My mate "Monty" was there, just grinning like a Cheshire Cat. I promised him that I would treat him to his favourite brand of pork pie next season, in celebration of City's promotion.

I found the enigmatic "Fletch", returning to his coach.

"Have you heard the England cricket score, Paul." he piped.

Whoever gave a Monkeys, Fletch. I ask you.

Graham came up behind Dave and I, and we had a group hug as well. Everybody was on Cloud Nine, and we would be buzzing for many weeks to come. It would be a gloriously happy journey home.

I was still thinking of my brother Neil and nephew Robert, who were listening halfway across the planet in the Philippines. They were here in 2009 and 2010, I could visualise them behind the goal.

LUTON TOWN: Tyler, Osano, Pilkington, Kovacs, Howell, Lawless, Keane, Watkins (J-P Kissock 61), Gray, Fleetwood (McAllister 61) (O'Connor 73), Willmott.

YORK CITY: Ingham, Challinor (Brown 37), Gibson, Parslow, Smith, Doig, Meredith, Oyebanjo, Walker (McLaughlin 86), Chambers (Reed 78), Blair.

Subs not used: Musselwhite, Moke.

CITY 2   LUTON 1   Attendance: 39,265.

Scorers: CITY; Chambers 26, Blair 47   **LUTON;** Gray 2.

I finally caught up with big John (Uttley), of the Harrogate Minster-Men as I had missed him on the way down.

"Well, John ,I tell you what, Neil (my brother), isn't very happy with you, mate"

"How's that, then Paul ?"

"Well, he thought you might have made a small detour to pick up the members of the Malaybalay (Philippines) Minstermen. It would only have been a 20,000 mile detour. Neil is a bit miffed."

Ah well, better luck next year, Neil and Rob. We'll get you there next time.

It was a happy bus ride back to Yorkshire,

"ANYONE FOR FISH AND CHIPS" ? ? ? ? ?

CHAPTER 15

CELEBRATION TIME

THERE had already been a minor celebration of City's FA Trophy victory on the evening of Tuesday, May the 15th. The players and manager of York City had stood on the steps of the Mansion House, in celebration of the club bringing home their first National Trophy in their 90-year-History, since their Midland League days.

The celebrations were purposely a low-key affair, as requested by Gary Mills, and the City Directors. At the time, everyone was hoping for the club to bring home the promotion play-off trophy, five days later, but nobody was counting their chickens at that time.

On a gloriously sunny evening, Monday May 21st, the play-off winners trophy had duly joined that other silverware in the Bootham Crescent Trophy cabinet, and now, the full scale party could begin, on City's night of glory. Both trophies were coming home to the wonderful City of York, and everybody was in the mood for a party.

We have done it. Mission accomplished. Wembley twice, and victorious on both occasions, and we were all still in 7th Heaven. The local press reports had been read over and over again, and the pictures taken still came to life before our eyes. This euphoric mood had to continue on and on. A second Civic Reception within 6 days had been organised within hours of the final whistle on that glorious Sunday, May 20th.

This time it was to be special; a celebration for the entire city of York and its people to enjoy. No need for tickets or packed lunches this time. The stage was set as the open-top bus set off from Bootham Crescent just before 6 pm. Players, staff and directors were crammed aboard the open deck of the bus, and they were soon hanging over the sides, and dancing with joy as they set off down Bootham Crescent, towards the City Centre.

Crowds had gathered in their hundreds to line the route, and many continued to follow the bus as it continued its journey. Within 15 minutes of leaving the ground, the procession had reached Blake Street, and on it went, past St Helen's Square, amidst a crescendo of clapping and cheering. The atmosphere was electric, and the players were visibly moved by it all. Onwards into Parliament Street, and as it turned into a packed Coney Street, the noise was growing ever louder, until the bus returned to St Helen's Square, and parked up at the Mansion House, its final destination.

Then the celebrations really began. A mass of swaying flags, and scarves, predominantly red and blue, in City's colours. Both trophies were held aloft, gleaming in the late afternoon sun. Each player took his turn to hold them up, and the biggest cheers had been reserved for manager Gary Mills. Matty Blair's famous long-lost dog was also to make a miraculous appearance. Spontaneous singing and chanting added to the joyous atmosphere of colour and occasion. The enormity of City's amazing achievements were just beginning to sink in now. Emotions were high, and everybody's day to day worries were swept away in a tide of dreams which had now come true at last, and became reality.

Everybody was "lost in the moment, and were all as one". The City of York was celebrating pride in its football club after many years of heartache and near misses. Everyone was happy and smiling, and nobody wanted this particular party to end.

By 6.50, most of the City party had left the bus, and were standing proudly on the very same steps where they had stood just 6 days earlier, at the Mansion House.

The final TV interviews on the bus were still being given, with reflections of the momentous events of the last 9 days. Everyone wished that the moment would last forever.

For everyone who followed the Minstermen during that, wonderful 2011-12 season, in particular those who went to Wembley, they would cherish the memories for a long time.

Just like old photographs, the memories can last forever, although the details may just fade around the edges after a while. In years to come they would just become a little piece of History in the inner reaches of our minds. But we all know that History cannot change.

There was nothing quite like being there

(Photographs on pages 185 to 190, courtesy of Mr Ted Clark).

City Celebrate their FA Trophy success.

Reception at the Mansion House, Tuesday May 15th.

Reception at the Mansion House, Tuesday May 15th.

ior to the play-off Final. City v Luton, Sunday May 20th.

Delighted Sophie Hicks with Matty Blair *(top)*
and manager Gary Mills *(bottom)*.

Top: City players and fans celebrate promotion.
Bottom: Gary Mills showing off both trophies at the Mansion House,
Monday May 21st.

At the Mansion House, Monday May 21st.

CHAPTER 16

YORK CITY'S PLAYERS, 2011-2012
PLAYER PROFILES

Notations; first figure is appearances in total, which includes appearances as substitute. Figures in brackets indicates number of goals scored. The figures include League and Cup games combined.

(L) indicates Loan spell at a club.

1. MOSES ASHIKODI: Born 27 June 1987, Lagos, Nigeria.
CAREER TO DATE: MILLWALL 2002-04   5 (0)
                                          WEST HAM 2004-06   0 (0)
                                          GILLINGHAM 2005-06   4 (0)
                                          RANGERS 2005-07   1 (0)
                                          WATFORD 2006-09   3 (1)
                                          BRADFORD C (L) 2006-07   8 (2)
                                          SWINDON T (L) 2007-08   10 (0)
                                          HEREFORD (L) 2008-09   3(1)
                                          SHREWSBURY T 2008-09   10 (1)
                                          KETTERING 2009-10   18 (8)
                                          EBBSFLEET 2009-10   16 (11)
                                          KETTERING 2010-12 25 (7)
                                          YORK CITY 2011-12   11 (1)

A journey-man footballer, Ashikodi's appearances in a City shirt were limited. He scored the last goal in the 7-0 drubbing of his mates from Kettering in December.

2. MATTY BLAIR: Born 5 July 1990, Warwick.

CAREER TO DATE:

REDDITCH U

AFC TELFORD } (Not known)

BEDWORTH U

KIDDERMINSTER 2010-11   43 (11)

YORK CITY 2011-12   52 (20)

Where do you start in summing up the season for our speedy winger/goalscorer supreme? He had a purple patch at the turn of the year, scoring 12 goals in 11 games. He scored the goal at Luton in the Trophy semi-final to get City to Wembley, and he scored the winner at Mansfield in the play-off semi-final to get us to Wembley again. Not happy with that, he scored the first goal at Wembley, in the final of the Trophy and the winner in the play-off Final against Luton at Wembley.

With all due respect to Scott Kerr, had the player of the season award been given at the end of May, I think Matty would have deserved a share of it as well.

3.   MATTHEW BLINKHORN: Born 2 March 1985, Blackpool.

CAREER TO DATE:

BLACKPOOL 2001-07   44 (5)

LUTON TOWN (L) 2004   2(0)

BURY 2006-07   10 (0)

MORECAMBE 2007-09   64 (18)

SLIGO ROVERS 2009-11   72 (22)

YORK CITY 2011-12   19 (2)

How vital was that last gasp winner against Stockport County in February at The Crescent? Matthew also scored with virtually his first touch in the 6-2 victory at Salisbury in the Trophy. He was a more than useful back-up striker.

4.   EUGEN BOPP: Born 5 September 1983, Kiev.

CAREER TO DATE: NOTTM FOREST 2001-06   89 (11)

                              ROTHERHAM U 2006-07   31 (5)

                              CREWE 2007-09   21 (2)

                              CARL ZEISS JENA   16 (0)

                              YORK CITY   2(0)

Unfortunate to be injured in his only start against Fleetwood, but played his part, in the comeback win at Luton in the League.

5.   ANDRE BOUCAUD: Born 10 October 1984, Enfield.

CAREER TO DATE: READING 2002-04   0 (0)

                              PETERBOROUGH 2002-06   42 (2)

                              ALDERSHOT (L) 2005-06   12 (0)

                              KETTERING 2006-07, 2008-11   164 (5)

                              WYCOMBE W 2007-08   11 (0)

                              YORK CITY 2011-12   45 (1)

                              LUTON TOWN 2011-12   7 (0)

                              TRINIDAD & TOBAGO, 6 FULL INTS

Sold to Luton in January, but was a useful cog in City's slick midfield unit in the early part of the season.

6.   SCOTT BROWN: Born 8 May 1985, Runcorn.

CAREER TO DATE: BRISTOL CITY 2004-07   71 (5)

                              CHELTENHAM 2006-09   21 (0)

                              PORT VALE 2008-09   12 (0)

                              MORECAMBE 2010-11   33 (3)

                              FLEETWOOD 2011-12   8 (0)

                              YORK CITY 2011-12   10 (0)

Brought in to replace Andre Boucaud in central midfield, he made a useful contribution from the bench at Luton, in the Trophy semi-final, and the play-off Final at Wembley, also as a substitute.

7.   JON CHALLINOR: Born 2 December 1980, Cambridge.

CAREER TO DATE: CAMBRIDGE CITY 2001-02   1 (0)

ST ALBANS 2002-03   1 (0)

ALDERSHOT 2003-05   85 (18)

EXETER C 2005-07   92 (21)

RUSHDEN/D 2007-08   50 (8)

CAMBRIDGE U 2008-11   39 (2)

FOREST GREEN 2009 (L)   6 (0)

MANSFIELD T 2009-10   20 (3)

NEWPORT C0 2010-11   2 (0)

KETTERING 2011-12   17(1)

YORK CITY 2011-12   51 (3)

A useful player with vast experience at Conference Level. But not for his last-gasp equaliser against Solihull in the FA Trophy, City would have been knocked out at the very first hurdle. Has played at right back, and on the wing for City this season.

8.   ASHLEY CHAMBERS: Born 1 March 1990, Leicester

CAREER TO DATE: LEICESTER C 2005-11   9 (0)

WYCOMBE W (L) 2009-10   4 (1)

GRIMSBY T (L) 2009-10   4 (2)

YORK CITY 2010-12   80 (13)

ENGLAND U/16   7 (3)

ENGLAND U/17   13 (7)

ENGLAND U/18   2 (0)

ENGLAND U/19   1 (0)

ENGLAND C   2 (0)

He struggled to find consistency at times, but remains City's main "assist" man for the season. Scored a delicious goal to bring City level in the play-off Final, and contributed 10 goals in all.

9.   CHRIS DOIG: Born 13 February 1981, Dumfries.

CAREER TO DATE:		
	QUEEN OF THE SOUTH 1996-97	4 (0)
	NOTTM FOREST 1997-2005	93 (1)
	NORTHAMPTON T 2003-2009	147 (5)
	CENTRAL COAST MARINERS	
	(Australia) 2009-11	26 (0)
	PELITA JAYA FC	
	(Indonesia) 2010-11	12 (0)
	ALDERSHOT T 2011-12	2 (0)
	YORK CITY	15 (0)
	SCOTLAND U/18	2 (0)
	SCOTLAND U/21	14 (0)

One of Gary Mills useful additions in the transfer window. A more than useful replacement for David McGurk, especially in the 3 play-off games.

10.   JAMAL FYFIELD: Born 17 March 1989.

CAREER TO DATE		
	MAIDENHEAD	(Not known)
	YORK CITY 2010-2012	54 (4)

Another versatile performer, who was at ease at full-back or in the centre of defence. Popped up with a timely equaliser against Mansfield in the dying seconds, and scored a priceless winner at Grimsby in the League victory. Supplied the perfect cross for Matty Blair to finish off Luton in the Trophy semi-final.

11.   BEN GIBSON: Born 15 January 1993, Nunthorpe.

CAREER TO DATE:		
	MIDDLESBROUGH 2011-12	1 (0)
	YORK CITY 2011-2012	11 (0)

Another transfer window addition to the City squad. Performed admirably in both Wembley Finals, considering he had only played a handful of games prior to those.

12.   LIAM HENDERSON: Born 28 December 1989, Gateshead.

CAREER TO DATE:		
	WATFORD 2007-11	21 (0)
	WEALDSTONE (L) 2007-08	10 (3)
	HARTLEPOOL (L) 2008-09	9 (0)
	COLCHESTER U (L) 2010-11	11 (0)
	ALDERSHOT (L) 2010-11	1 (0)
	ROTHERHAM (L) 2010-11	11 (0)
	FOREST GREEN (L) 2011-12	22 (2)
	YORK CITY 2011-12	7 (1)

Managed a goal, against Mansfield, in between his loan spells at Forest Green. His chances were limited.

13.   MICHAEL INGHAM: Born 9 July 1980, Preston.

CAREER TO DATE:	
	CLIFTONVILLE 1998-1999 35
	SUNDERLAND 1999-2005 4
	CARLISLE (L) 1999-2000 7
	CLIFTONVILLE (L) 2000-2001 20
	STOKE CITY (L) 2001-02 0
	STOCKPORT (L) 2002-03 1
	DARLINGTON (L) 2002-03 3
	YORK CITY (L) 2002-03 17
	WREXHAM (L) 2003-04 11
	DONCASTER R (L) 2004-05 2
	WREXHAM 2005-07 80
	HEREFORD U 2007-08 1
	YORK CITY 2008-12 213
	N. IRELAND 3 Full caps

Highly experienced keeper, one of the best in the Conference. Had nerveless games in both Wembley Finals after a nervous time there in 2010. A reliable and confident performer all season.

14.   REECE KELLY: One appearance for City in the final game against Forest Green for the first year apprentice.

15.   SCOTT KERR; Born 11 December 1981, Leeds.

CAREER TO DATE:	BRADFORD C 1999-2001	3 (0)
	HULL CITY 2001-03	1 (0)
	FRICKLEY (L) 2002-03	?
	SCARBOROUGH 2002-05	97 (4)
	LINCOLN C 2005-11	248 (9)
	YORK CITY 2011-12	58 (1)

A non-stop runner in the Anchor role in midfield. Deservedly won the player of the season award for his energy levels and total dedication to the cause. His only goal of the season put City into the semi-finals of the FA Trophy.

16.   DAVID McGURK: Born 30 September 1982, Middlesbrough

CAREER TO DATE:	DARLINGTON 2001-06	63 (6)
	YORK CITY 2004-2012	296 (5)

A loyal servant to the club for 6 years, after originally joining on loan from Darlington. Turned down a move to Luton Town, but sadly his season was ended by injury in January.

17.   PADDY McLAUGHLIN: Born 14 January 1991, Larne.

CAREER TO DATE:	NEWCASTLE U 2008-11	0 (0)
	YORK CITY 2011-12	55 (13)
	N IRELAND U/21	5 (0)

An absolute Magician in midfield, and a brilliant free-kick taker. Only missed two League games all season, and made 16 assists. A most valuable performer who contributed 13 goals as well.

18.　JAMES MEREDITH: Born 4 April 1988, Albury, Australia.

CAREER TO DATE:　　　　DERBY COUNTY 2006-07　0 (0)

CAMBRIDGE U (L) 2006-07　2 (0)

CHESTERFIELD (L) 2006-07　1 (0)

SLIGO ROVERS 2007　4 (0)

SHREWSBURY 2007-09　3 (0)

TELFORD (L) 2008-09　45 (1)

YORK CITY 2010-2012　162 (3)

Another versatile performer, at ease at full-back or in midfield. Scored the amazing winner at Luton in the League to give City a remarkable victory. Would be a shame to lose him in the close season.

19.　ADRIANO MOKE: Born 11 January 1990, Portugal.

CAREER TO DATE:　　　　JEREZ INDUSTRIAL (Spain)

YORK CITY　34 (3)

A product of the Glenn Hoddle Academy in Spain, he found it difficult to make many starts in view of the talented wingers in the squad. Did score the brilliant, last goal against Braintree, and the final goal of City's League season.

20.　PAUL MUSSELWHITE, Born 22 December 1968, Portsmouth.

CAREER TO DATE:　　　　SCUNTHORPE 1987-1992　163

PORT VALE 1992-2000　367

SHEFFIELD W 2000-2001　0

HULL CITY 2000-2004　104

SCUNTHORPE 2004-2006　82

EASTLEIGH 2006-07　8

KETTERING 2006-07　3

HARROGATE TOWN 2007-08　13

GATESHEAD 2007-09　71

LINCOLN CITY 2009-2011　1

YORK CITY 2011-12　3

A veteran, and a record breaker for City, being the oldest player to represent the club, and to keep a clean sheet in his all of his first and only three appearances for the club.

21.   LANRE OYEBANJO: Born 27 April 1990, London.

CAREER TO DATE:	BRENTFORD 2008 0(0)
	HISTON 2008-11 112 (3)
	YORK CITY 2011-12 27 (3)
	EIRE U/21 6 (0)

Yet another utility player, comfortable at full-back or in midfield. Scored against Alfreton and Hayes, plus the brilliant second goal against Newport in the FA Trophy Final. Made two magnificent blocks against Luton at Wembley, late on, to protect our play-off lead.

22.   DANNY PARSLOW: Born 11 September 1985, Hengoed, Wales

CAREER TO DATE:	CARDIFF CITY 2005-09 0 (0)
	YORK CITY 2006-2012 249 (3)
	WALES U/17 1
	WALES U/19 3
	WALES U/21 4
	WALES SEMI-PRO 3

Second longest serving player to David McGurk. Responded well to his new role as Anchor man towards the end of the season, after Scott Kerr's injury.

23.   DANNY PILKINGTON: Born 25 May 1990, Blackburn.

| CAREER TO DATE: | STOCKPORT CO 2008-11   38 (1) |
| | YORK CITY 2011-12   22 (2) |

Drifted in and out of the City team, with the competition from City's many wide players. Scored the last of 5 at Kettering in his first appearance, off the bench.

24.   MICHAEL POTTS: Born 26 November 1991, Blackburn.

CAREER TO DATE: BLACKBURN R 2008-11   0 (0)

                               YORK CITY 2011-12   12 (0)

A young player, full of promise for the future. Showed superb long-range passing skills in his limited appearances this season.

25.   JAMIE REED: Born 13 August 1987, Connah's Quay, Wales.

CAREER TO DATE: WREXHAM 2005-08   7 (0)

                               GLENTORAN (L) 2005-06   5 (0)

                               COLWYN BAY (L) 2006   5 (4)

                               ABERYSTWYTH T (L) 2007-8   20 (9)

                               TAMWORTH (L) 2007-08   11 (1)

                               RHYL 2008-09   31 (13)

                               BANGOR CITY 2009-11   61 (48)

                               DANDENONG THUNDER (L) 2010   7 (5)

                               YORK CITY 2011-12   66 (21)

Popular with most of the City faithful, having made many useful contributions coming off the bench, and scoring a clutch of late points-saving goals. Sadly did not get much of a chance to show his goal-poaching skills at either of the Wembley matches.

26.   CHRIS SMITH: Born 30 June 1981, Derby.

CAREER TO DATE: READING 2000-01   0 (0)

                               YORK CITY 2001-04   88 (0)

                               STAFFORD R 2004-05   23 (1)

                               WORCESTER C 2005-8   121 (12)

                               TAMWORTH 2008-10   80 (6)

                               MANSFIELD T 2010   15 (1)

                               YORK CITY 2010-2012   71 (5)

City's Captain for most of the season, in his second spell with the club. Was prone to mistakes early in the season, but came back strong and solid when required at the "Business" end of the season.

27.   BEN SWALLOW: Born 20 October 1989, Barry.

CAREER TO DATE:	BRISTOL R 2008-12	49 (2)
	TAUNTON (L) 2008-9	5 (0)
	BATH CITY (L) 2011-12	9 (0)
	YORK CITY 2011-12	3 (0)

Hardly had the chance to make much of an impact at City, but looked promising ,with some neat touches.

28.   ERIK TONNE: Born 7 May 1991, Trondheim, Norway.

CAREER TO DATE:	SHEFFIELD U 2010-2012	6 (2)
	YORK CITY 2011-12	4 (1)

Not much of a chance to shine, but he scored a vital goal at Braintree to give City the victory they needed to make the play-offs.

29.   JASON WALKER: Born 21 February 1984, Barrow-in-Furness.

CAREER TO DATE:	MORTON 2004-07	92 (17)
	MORECAMBE 2006-07	7 (1)
	BARROW 2006-10	175 (64)
	LUTON TOWN 2010-11	29 (6)
	YORK CITY 2011-12	39 (18)
	ENGLAND 'C'	1 (0)

City's Talisman Striker, and scorer of the best goal seen at Bootham Crescent for many years. A skillful, versatile striker who also holds the ball up well for others. But not for his mid-season injury, he would have scored a lot more goals. Well worth the £60k City forked out for him.

THE MANAGER, GARY MILLS: Born 11 November 1961, Northampton.
CAREER PROFILE AS A PLAYER:

	NOTTM FOREST 1978-82	58 (8)
	SEATTLE 1982-83	34 (5)
	DERBY CO (L) 1982-83	18 (2)
	NOTTM FOREST 1983-87	78 (4)
	NOTTS COUNTY 1987-89	75 (8)
	LEICESTER C 1989-94	200 (15)
	NOTTS COUNTY 1994-96	47(0)
AS PLAYER-MANAGER:	GRANTHAM T	July 96 - May 98
	KINGS LYNN	Sep 98 - Nov 2000
	TAMWORTH	Jan 2001 - May 2002
	NOTTS COUNTY	Jan 2004 - Nov 2004
	ALFRETON T	May 2005 - Jan 2007
	TAMWORTH	Jan 2007 - Oct 2010
MANAGER:	YORK CITY	from 13 Oct 2010

GARY MILLS was a player in the Nottingham Forest, European Cup-winning team under Brian Clough in 1979-80. As a player he had 2 spells at both Forest and County, before going on to player-manage several non-league clubs. He led Tamworth to a comfortable mid-table position in the National Conference, before moving to York City on October 13th, 2010.

We have never looked back.

BLUE SQUARE NATIONAL CONFERENCE
FINAL TABLE 2011-2012

1.	Fleetwood T	46	13	8	2	50-25	18	2	3	52-23	103
2.	Wrexham	46	16	3	4	48-17	14	5	4	37-16	98
3.	Mansfield T	46	14	6	3	50-25	11	8	4	37-23	89
4.	YORK CITY	46	11	6	6	43-24	12	8	3	38-21	83
5.	Luton Town.	46	15	4	4	48-15	7	11	5	30-27	81
6.	Kidderminster	46	10	7	6	44-32	12	3	8	38-31	76
7.	Southport	46	8	8	7	36-39	13	5	5	36-30	76
8.	Gateshead	46	11	8	4	39-26	10	3	10	30-36	74
9.	Cambridge U	46	11	6	6	31-16	8	8	7	26-25	71
10.	Forest Green	46	11	5	7	37-25	8	8	7	29-20	70
11.	Grimsby Town	46	12	4	7	51-28	7	9	7	28-32	70
12.	Braintree T	46	11	5	7	39-34	6	6	11	37-46	62
13.	Barrow	46	12	6	5	39-25	5	3	15	23-51	60
14.	Ebbsfleet Utd	46	7	6	10	34-39	7	6	10	35-45	54
15.	Alfreton T	46	8	6	9	39-48	7	3	13	23-38	54
16.	Stockport Co	46	8	7	8	35-28	4	8	11	23-46	51
17.	Lincoln City	46	8	6	9	32-24	5	4	14	24-42	49
18.	Tamworth	46	7	9	7	30-30	4	6	13	17-40	48
19.	Newport Co	46	8	6	9	22-22	3	8	12	31-43	47
20.	AFC Telford	46	9	6	8	24-26	1	10	12	21-39	46
21.	Hayes/Yeading	46	5	5	13	26-41	6	3	14	32-49	41
22.	Darlington	46	8	7	8	24-24	3	6	14	23-49	36
23.	Bath City	46	5	4	14	27-41	2	6	15	16-48	31
24.	Kettering	46	5	5	13	25-47	3	4	16	15-53	30

Darlington were deducted 10 pts, Kettering 3 pts.

RESULTS AND SCORERS (1)   AUG-DEC 2011

	2011		OPPONENTS	RES	ATT	SCORERS		POS
1	Aug 13	A	Ebbsfleet	W 2-1	1522	Walker (Pen) 83, 90+2	C	5
2	Aug 16	H	BARROW	W 3-1	3075	Walker 7, McLaughlin 45+2 Blair 90 is	C	2
3	Aug 20	H	AFC TELFORD	L 0-1	2723		C	5
4	Aug 23	A	Kettering	W 5-1	1595	Boucaud 20, Walker 21.31 Moke 39 Pilkington 90	C	3
5	Aug 26	A	Fleetwood T	D 0-0	2111		C	3
6	Aug 29	H	ALFRETON T	L 0-1	3166		C	6
7	Sep 10	A	Tamworth	L 1-2	1012	Walker 84	C	14
8	Sep 13	H	BATH CITY	W 1-0	2030	Reed 88	C	9
9	Sep 17	A	Wrexham	W 3-0	3872	McLaughlin 4, Chambers 21. Reed 24	C	8
10	Sep 20	H	DARLINGTON	D 2-2	2834	Reed 2, Walker 79	C	7
11	Sep 24	H	LUTON TOWN	W 3-0	3570	Chambers 9, 45 Walker 31	C	5
12	Sep 27	A	Gateshead	L 2-3	1604	Walker 23, Curtis (og) 87	C	8
13	Oct 1	A	Stockport	W 2-1	3753	Blair 52, Walker 86	C	6
14	Oct 8	H	BRAINTREE	W 6-2	2640	Chambers 15, McLaughlin 28, 41 Fyfield 37 Walker (Pen) 72. Moke 85	C	4
15	Oct 11	A	Southport	D 1-1	1107	Chambers 62	C	4
16	Oct 15	H	GRIMSBY T	W 2-1	3872	Walker 34, Chambers 86	C	3
17	Oct 18	H	CAMBRIDGE	D 2-2	2711	Walker 21, 89	C	3
18	Oct 22	A	Hayes/Yead	W 4-2	525	Walker 14, Challinor 19 McLaughlin 62, Chambers 76	C	3
19	Oct 29	A	Wrexham	L 1-2	2252	McLaughlin 58	F	
20	Nov 5	H	WREXHAM	D 0-0	4295		C	4
21	Nov 19	A	Barrow	D 0-0	2190		C	5
22	Nov 26	A	Forest Green	D 1-1	1157	Reed (Pen) 83	C	5
23	Nov 29	H	LINCOLN C	W 2-0	3155	Pilkington 4, McLaughlin 56	C	4
24	Dec 3	H	KETTERING	W 7-0	2899	Reed 6, 12 Challinor 30, Blair 45+3 McLaughlin 50, Chambers 65, Ashikodi 77	C	4
25	Dec 6	A	AFC Telford	D 0-0	1601		C	3
26	Dec 10	H	Solihull M	D 2-2	1116	Blair 6, Challinor 90+3	T	
27	Dec 13	A	Solihull M	W 3-0	275	Smith 11, Blair 62, 77	T	
28	Dec 19	H	KIDDERMINSTER	L 2-3	2830	Blair 20, McGurk 67	C	4
29	Dec 26	A	Mansfield T	D 1-1	3551	Henderson 63	C	4

*KEY TO COMPETITIONS:-

C = CONFERENCE   F = FA CUP   T = FA TROPHY

RESULTS AND SCORERS (2)   JAN-MAY 2012

	2012		OPPONENTS	RES	ATT	SCORERS	POS	
30	JAN 1	H	MANSFIELD T	D 2-2	4284	Blair 77, Fyfield 90+1	C	5
31	Jan 7	A	Lincoln C	W 2-0	3048	Blair 64, 72	C	4
32	Jan 14	A	Salisbury C	W 6-2	827	Blair 19, 21 Reed 26, McLaughlin 34, 87 Blinkhorn 70	T	
33	JAN 21	H	EBBSFLEET U	W 3-2	2973	Blair 10, 52 Meredith 67	C	4
34	Jan 24	A	Kidderminster	D 1-1	2417	Smith 57	C	4
35	Jan 28	A	Darlington	D 2-2	643	Smith 60, Chambers 61	C	4
36	FEB 14	H	EBBSFLEET U	W 1-0	1419	Blair 48	T	
37	FEB 18	H	STOCKPORT CO	W 2-1	3370	Reed 84, Blinkhorn 90+6	C	4
38	FEB 22	H	GATESHEAD	L 1-2	2683	Reed 65	C	4
39	Feb 25	A	Grimsby T	W 1-0	3662	Kerr 83	T	
40	MAR 3	H	HAYES/YEAD	W 2-0	2603	Oyebanjo 57, Walker (Pen) 90+2	C	4
41	MAR 6	H	TAMWORTH	D 0-0	2249		C	4
42	MAR 10	H	LUTON TOWN	W 1-0	3365	Reed (Pen) 14	T	
43	Mar 13	A	Grimsby T	W 3-2	4250	Reed 19, Smith 47, Fyfield 90+3	C	5
44	Mar 17	A	Luton Town	D 1-1	5796	Blair 90	T	
45	MAR 24	H	SOUTHPORT	L 1-2	3465	Reed 84	C	6
46	Mar 27	A	Bath City	W 1-0	565	McLaughlin 50	C	5
47	Mar 30	A	Luton Town	W 2-1	5925	McLaughlin 80, Meredith 86	C	4
48	Apr 3	A	Newport Co	L 1-2	1241	McLaughlin 39	C	4
49	APR 7	H	FLEETWOOD T	L 0-1	4048		C	4
50	Apr 9	A	Alfreton T	W 2-0	1603	Blair 69, Oyebanjo 76	C	4
51	APR 14	H	NEWPORT CO	D 1-1	2824	Walker 59	C	5
52	Apr 17	A	Cambridge U	W 1-0	2211	Walker 65	C	4
53	APR 21	A	Braintree	W 1-0	1129	Tonne 75	C	4
54	APR 28	H	FOREST GREEN	W 1-0	3391	Moke 82	C	4
55	MAY 2	H	MANSFIELD T	D 1-1	6057	Geohaghon (og) 42	P	
56	May 7	A	Mansfield T	W 1-0*	7295	Blair 111	P	
57	MAY 12	W	NEWPORT CO	W 2-0	19,844	Blair 65, Oyebanjo 72	T	
58	MAY 20	W	LUTON TOWN	W 2-1	39,265	Chambers 26, Blair 47	P	

P = PLAY-OFFS   W = At WEMBLEY STADIUM   * AFTER EXTRA TIME

LINE-UPS: (1) AUG-DEC 2011

(S) = CAME ON AS SUB

#	Opp	V	Ingham (24)	Oyebanjo (2)	Meredith (3)	Moke (18)	McGurk (5)	Smith (4)	Gougaud (15)	McLaughlin (26)	Walker (9)	Chambers (10)	Blair (17)	Parslow (6)	Reed (7)	Potts (14)	Fyfield (16)	Henderson (11)	Kerr (8)	Pilkington (12)	Challinor (20)	Mashikodi (28)
1	EBB	A	1	2	3	4	5	6	7	8	9	10	11									
2	BAR	H	1	2	3	4	5	6	7	8	9	10	11	(S)	(S)							
3	TEL	H	1	2	3	4	5	6	7	8	9	10	11	(S)			(S)			(S)		
4	KET	A	1	2	3	11	5	6	7	8	9	10		(S)			(S)			4	(S)	
5	FLE	A	1	2	3	11	5	6	7	8	9	10					(S)			4	(S)	(S)
6	ALF	H	1		3	11	5	6	7	8	9	10		2	(S)		(S)			4		(S)
7	TAM	A	1	2	3	8	5	6		(S)	9	10	11		(S)				(S)	4	7	
8	BAT	H	1		3		5		8		9	10	(S)	2	(S)		6	(S)		4	11	7
9	WRE	A	1		3		5		7	8	9	10	(S)			11		(S)	6	4		2
10	DAR	H	1		3	(S)	5		7	8	9	10	11				6			4		2
11	LUT	H	1		3	(S)	5		7	8	9	10	(S)			11	6	(S)		4		2
12	GAT	A	1		3	(S)	5		7	8	9	10	(S)			11	6	(S)		4		2
13	STO	A	1		3		5		7	8	9	10	11	(S)	(S)		6			4		2
14	BRA	H	1		3	(S)	5		7	8	9	10	11	(S)	(S)		6			4		2
15	SOU	A	1		3		5		7	8	9	10	11			(S)	6			4		2
16	GRI	H	1		3	(S)	5		7	8	9	10	11			(S)	6			4		2
17	CAM	H	1		3	(S)	5		7	8	9	10	11	(S)	(S)		6			4		2
18	HAY	A	1		3	(S)	5		7	8	9	10	11	(S)	(S)		6			4		2
19	WRE	A	1	2	3	11	5			8		(S)	(S)	6	10	7		9		4		(S)
20	WRE	H	1		3	(S)	5		7	8	9	10	11			(S)	6			4		2
21	BAR	A	1		3	(S)	5		7	8	9	10	11	(S)			6			4	(S)	2
22	FOR	A	1	2	3		5			8		10	11	(S)	(S)		6		(S)	4	7	9
23	LIN	H	1	(S)	3		5			8		10	11		9		6			4	7	2
24	KET	H	1	(S)	3	(S)	5			8		10	11		9		6			4	7	2
25	TEL	A	1		3		5		7	8	9	10	11	(S)			6			4	(S)	2
26	SOL	H	1		3	(S)	5		7	8	9		11			(S)	6			4	10	2
27	SOL	A	1			11	5	4		8	9	10	3				6			(S)	7	2
28	KID	H	1		3	(S)	5		7	8		10	11	(S)			6			4	9	2
29	MAN	A	1	2	3		5	6		8		(S)	11	10	(S)	7		9		4		

NB. THE NUMBERS ALLOCATED TO PLAYERS ARE MY OWN INTERPRETATION AS TO HOW THE TEAMS LINED UP. SQUAD NUMBERS IN BRACKETS *

LINE-UPS (2)   JAN-MAY 2012

#			M.INGHAM (24)	LOYEBANJO (2)	J.MEREDITH (3)	A.MOKE (18)	D.MCGURK (5)	C.SMITH (4)	P.MCLAUGHLIN (26)	J.WALKER (4)	A.CHAMBERS (10)	M.BLAIR (11)	D.PARSLOW (6)	J.REED (7)	M.POTTS (14)	J.FYFIELD (16)	S.KERR (8)	D.PILKINGTON (12)	J.CHALLINOR (20)	M.ASHIKODI (28)	S.BROWN (19)	M.BLINKHORN (21)	C.DOIG (23)	E.TONNE (15)	B.GIBSON (27)	E.BOPP (13)	P.MUSSELWHITE (1)
30	MAN	H	1	2	3		5		8		10	11	6	(S)	7	(S)	4	(S)					9				
31	LIN	A	1		3		5		8		(S)	10	6	9			4	11	2	(S)	7	(S)	L.HENDERSON				
32	SAL	A	1		3	(S)	5		8			10	6	9			4	11	2	(S)	7	(S)	L.HENDERSON				
33	EBB	H	1		3		5		8			10	6	9		(S)	4	11	2		7		L.HENDERSON				
34	KID	A	1		3	7	5		8		(S)	10	6	9	(S)		4	11	2			(S)	L.HENDERSON				
35	DAR	A	1		3		5		8		(S)	10	6	(S)	7	(S)	4	11	2				9				
36	EBB	H	1		3		5		8	9	(S)	10	(S)	(S)	A.BOUCAUD		4		2				6	7		11	
37	STO	H	1				5		8	9	10	11	(S)				4		2		7	(S)	6		3	(S)	
38	GAT	H	1				5		8	9	10	11	(S)				4		2		7	(S)	6		3	(S)	
39	GRI	A	1	2	7	(S)	5		8	9	10	11					4		(S)		(S)	6	6		3		
40	HAY	H	1	2	3	(S)			8	9	10	11	(S)				4		7		(S)	6	6		5		
41	TAM	H	1	2	3				8	9	10	11	6	(S)		5	4	(S)	7		(S)						
42	LUT	H	1	7	8		5			(S)		6	9	(S)	3	4	(S)	2	11		10						
43	GRI	A	1		7		5	8	9		11	6	10				3	4		2		(S)	(S)			B.SWALLOW	
44	LUT	A	1		7		5	8	9	(S)	11	6	10				3	4		2		(S)	(S)				
45	SOU	H	1	8	7	(S)	5	(S)	10	11	6	9			3				2		(S)			4			
46	BAT	A	1	7	3	(S)	5	8	10	11	(S)	9							2	4	(S)	6					
47	LUT	A	1	4	7		5	8	9	(S)	11	(S)	10						2		(S)		6		3	(S)	
48	NEW	A	1		7	(S)		8	(S)	11	5	9		3					2	(S)	10		6				
49	FLE	H	1	2	7	(S)		8	(S)	11	5	9							(S)		6	10	3	4			
50	ALF	A	1	2	3	11	5	8		10		9		(S)	R.KELLY		7	(S)			(S)	6					
51	NEW	H	1	2	3	11	5	8	(S)	(S)	10	4	9		R.KELLY		7	(S)			6				3		1
52	CAM	A		4	7		5	8	9	10	11	(S)		(S)	R.KELLY			2		(S)	(S)		6		3		1
53	BRA	A			7		5	8	9	10	11	6		4	3		R.KELLY	2	(S)	(S)		(S)					1
54	FOR	H			11							6	(S)	8	3	(S)	(S)	2	10	4	5	7					1
55	MAN	H	1		7	(S)	5	8	9	10	11	4		3					2		6						
56	MAN	A	1	7	3	(S)	5	8	9	10	11	4		(S)	(S)				2		6						
57	NEW	W	1	4	7	(S)	5	8	9	10	11	6	(S)		(S)				2				3				
58	LUT	W	1	8	7		5	(S)	9	10	11	4	(S)						2		(S)		6		3		

W = At WEMBLEY STADIUM

APPEARANCES AND GOALS + (SUBS)

SQUAD No	CONF. APPS	GLS	PLAY-OFFS APPS	GLS	TROPHY APPS	GLS	FA CUP APPS	GLS	TOTAL APPS	GLS
28 Moses Ashikodi	2+6 (1)								3+8 (1)	
17 Matty Blair	37+4 (10)		3	(2)	7	(8)	0+1		47+5 (20)	
21 Matthew Blinkhorn	3+12 (1)				1+3 (1)				4+15 (2)	
13 Eugen Bopp	1+1								1+1	
15 Andre Boucaud	23+1 (1)				1				24+1 (1)	
19 Scott Brown	6+1		0+1		1+1				7+3	
20 Jon Challinor	35+4 (2)		3		7+1 (1)		0+1		45+6 (3)	
10 Ashley Chambers	34+8 (9)		3	(1)	2+3		0+1		39+12 (10)	
23 Chris Doig	10		3		2				15	
16 Jamal Fyfield	25+8 (3)		1+1		4+1				30+10 (3)	
27 Ben Gibson	8		1		2				11	
12 Liam Henderson	2+4 (1)						1		3+4 (1)	
24 Michael Ingham	43		3		8		1		55	
25 Reece Kelly	0+1								0+1	
8 Scott Kerr *	33+1				7	(1)	1		41+1 (1)	
26 Patrick McLaughlin	42+2 (10)		2+1		7	(2)	1	(1)	52+3 (13)	
5 David McGurk	18+1 (1)				2		1		21+1 (1)	
3 James Meredith	43 (2)		3		8		1		55 (2)	
18 Adriano Moke	11+15 (3)		0+2		0+5		1		12+22 (3)	
1 Paul Musselwhite	3								3	
2 Lanre Oyebanjo	19+2 (2)		2		3	(1)	1		25+2 (3)	
6 Danny Parslow	17+10		3		5+2		1		26+12	
12 Danny Pilkington	10+8 (2)				2+2				12+10 (2)	
14 Michael Potts	2+8		0+1		0+1		1		3+10	
7 Jamie Reed	17+18 (10)		0+1		3+2 (2)		1		21+21 (12)	
4 Chris Smith	31 (3)		3		7	(1)			41 (4)	
22 Ben Swallow	0+2				1				1+2	
15 Erik Tonne	2+1 (1)				1				3+1 (1)	
9 Jason Walker	29+1 (18)		3		6				38+1 (18)	

o.g ~1   o.g ~1   TOTAL: 103 GOALS

* PLAYER OF THE SEASON

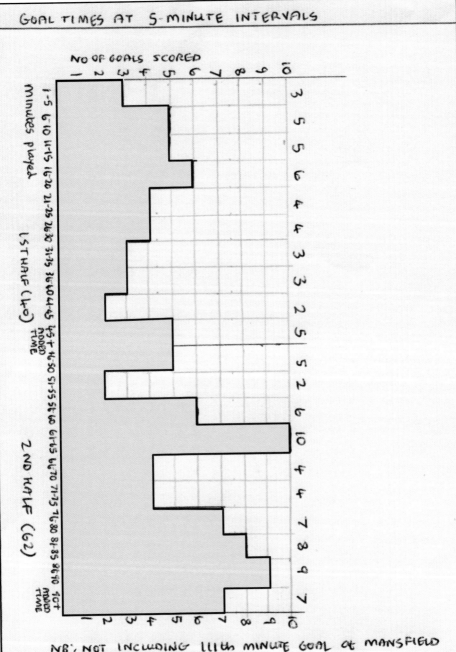

GOAL TIMES AT 5-MINUTE INTERVALS

NB: NOT INCLUDING 111th MINUTE GOAL of MANSFIELD
∴ 31 GOALS SCORED AFTER THE 75th MINUTE

BLUE SQUARE CONFERENCE RESULTS ; 2011-2012 (1)

HOME TEAMS \ AWAY TEAMS	AFC TELFORD	ALFRETON T	BARROW	BATH CITY	BRAINTREE T	CAMBRIDGE U	DARLINGTON	EBBSFLEET U	FLEETWOOD T	FOREST GREEN	GATESHEAD	GRIMSBY T
AFC TELFORD		1-0	1-0	2-1	1-0	1-2	3-3	0-2	1-4	2-0	1-2	0-0
ALFRETON T	0-0		2-1	2-1	0-1	2-1	3-1	2-2	1-4	1-6	1-1	2-5
BARROW	2-1	1-0		0-1	0-4	1-3	3-0	1-1	4-0	1-1	1-2	2-2
BATH CITY	3-1	0-3	0-1		1-1	3-4	2-0	2-3	1-4	0-2	4-2	2-2
BRAINTREE T	2-1	1-2	1-0	3-3		3-2	3-1	2-3	1-2	1-5	3-1	5-0
CAMBRIDGE U	1-0	3-0	1-0	1-1	2-0		2-0	2-0	2-0	1-1	0-1	0-1
DARLINGTON	1-0	1-1	0-1	2-2	1-0	2-0		0-2	0-1	0-0	0-1	0-0
EBBSFLEET U	3-2	1-2	1-2	3-0	1-1	0-0	1-3		1-3	1-1	0-1	3-1
FLEETWOOD T	2-2	4-0	4-1	4-1	3-1	1-0	0-0	6-2		0-0	3-1	2-1
FOREST GREEN	2-1	4-1	3-0	3-0	0-2	2-1	2-0	3-1	1-2		2-1	0-1
GATESHEAD	3-0	2-0	2-0	1-0	2-2	1-1	1-1	2-3	1-1	1-0		1-0
GRIMSBY T	2-0	5-2	5-2	6-0	1-1	2-1	1-2	4-3	0-2	2-1	2-0	
HAYES/YEADING	0-0	3-1	1-1	1-1	1-2	0-0	3-2	1-2	1-3	2-0	2-3	1-2
KETTERING	2-1	0-2	1-1	1-1	2-1	0-0	0-0	2-2	2-3	1-3	2-1	1-2
KIDDERMINSTER	2-2	3-1	1-2	4-1	5-4	0-0	3-1	2-2	0-2	1-0	2-3	1-1
LINCOLN C	1-1	0-1	2-1	2-0	3-3	0-1	5-0	3-0	1-3	1-1	1-0	1-2
LUTON TOWN	1-1	1-0	5-1	2-0	3-1	0-1	2-0	3-0	1-2	1-1	5-1	1-1
MANSFIELD T	1-1	3-2	7-0	1-1	4-1	1-2	5-2	1-0	1-1	1-0	1-1	2-1
NEWPORT CO	0-0	1-0	2-2	1-0	3-4	0-1	0-0	0-1	0-1	0-0	1-0	0-0
SOUTHPORT	3-2	2-1	2-1	2-1	0-4	1-0	2-0	3-3	0-6	1-3	1-3	1-2
STOCKPORT CO	2-2	0-0	3-2	4-0	1-1	0-1	3-4	1-1	2-4	0-1	0-1	2-0
TAMWORTH	2-2	2-2	2-3	0-1	1-0	2-2	1-0	1-0	0-3	0-1	1-1	1-1
WREXHAM	4-0	0-1	2-0	2-0	5-1	1-1	2-1	1-0	2-0	1-2	2-1	2-2
YORK CITY	0-1	0-1	3-1	1-0	6-2	2-2	2-2	3-2	0-1	1-0	1-2	2-1

BLUE SQUARE CONFERENCE RESULTS : 2011 - 2012   (2)

HOME TEAMS \ AWAY TEAMS	HAYES/YEADING	KETTERING	KIDDERMINSTER	LINCOLN C	LUTON TOWN	MANSFIELD T	NEWPORT CO	SOUTHPORT	STOCKPORT CO	TAMWORTH	WREXHAM	YORK CITY
AFC TELFORD	1-1	3-1	2-1	1-2	0-2	0-0	2-1	0-1	1-1	1-0	0-2	0-0
ALFRETON T	3-2	1-1	0-2	1-3	0-0	3-6	3-2	0-0	6-1	5-2	1-4	0-2
BARROW	3-1	3-0	3-1	1-0	1-0	2-3	3-1	2-2	1-0	1-1	3-1	0-0
BATH CITY	0-1	0-1	1-2	2-1	1-1	1-1	3-2	1-2	0-2	0-2	0-2	0-1
BRAINTREE T	0-3	2-1	1-4	1-0	3-1	1-1	1-0	0-0	2-2	3-1	0-0	0-1
CAMBRIDGE U	2-1	2-0	1-2	2-0	1-1	1-2	1-1	3-0	2-2	0-1	1-1	0-1
DARLINGTON	1-1	3-1	1-0	3-1	1-1	0-2	2-0	0-3	0-1	2-0	2-4	2-2
EBBSFLEET U	3-1	1-0	3-3	2-3	2-2	0-3	1-1	1-2	2-1	3-0	0-5	1-2
FLEETWOOD T	1-0	3-0	5-2	2-2	0-2	2-0	1-4	2-2	2-1	2-2	1-1	0-0
FOREST GREEN	1-3	0-1	1-1	0-2	3-0	1-1	1-1	2-3	1-1	3-1	1-0	1-1
GATESHEAD	2-0	1-1	2-1	3-3	0-0	3-0	2-3	2-3	2-0	1-1	1-4	3-2
GRIMSBY T	3-0	2-1	1-2	3-1	0-1	0-0	2-2	0-1	7-0	0-0	1-3	2-3
HAYES/YEADING		1-0	1-3	1-2	2-2	1-3	0-4	0-2	1-2	1-0	0-2	2-4
KETTERING	3-5		0-1	1-0	0-5	0-3	3-2	2-3	1-3	0-2	0-1	1-5
KIDDERMINSTER	3-1	6-1		1-1	1-2	0-3	3-2	2-0	1-1	2-0	0-1	1-1
LINCOLN C	0-1	0-2	0-1		1-1	1-1	2-0	2-0	1-1	4-0	1-2	0-2
LUTON TOWN	4-2	5-0	1-0	1-0		0-0	2-0	5-1	1-0	3-0	0-1	1-2
MANSFIELD T	3-2	3-0	0-3	2-1	1-1		5-0	1-3	2-1	2-1	2-0	1-1
NEWPORT CO	4-0	3-1	1-3	1-0	0-1	1-0		0-3	1-1	1-2	0-1	2-1
SOUTHPORT	1-2	0-0	1-2	2-2	3-3	3-1	1-1		5-0	1-1	0-0	1-1
STOCKPORT CO	3-3	1-0	2-1	4-0	1-1	0-1	2-2	0-1		2-0	1-0	1-2
TAMWORTH	2-1	2-2	0-0	4-0	1-3	0-1	2-1	2-2	1-1		1-2	2-1
WREXHAM	4-1	4-1	2-0	2-0	2-0	1-3	0-0	2-0	4-0	3-0		0-3
YORK CITY	2-0	7-0	2-3	2-0	3-0	2-2	1-1	1-2	2-1	0-0	0-0	

BLUE SQUARE CONFERENCE 2011-12 — ATTENDANCES (1)

Home Teams \ Away Teams	AFC TELFORD	ALFRETON	BARROW	BATH CITY	BRAINTREE T	CAMBRIDGE U	DARLINGTON	EBBSFLEET U	FLEETWOOD	FOREST GREEN	GATESHEAD	GRIMSBY T
AFC TELFORD		1871	1814	2093	1776	1903	1908	2004	2313	1674	2484	2676
ALFRETON	940		678	786	656	965	950	661	625	626	651	1924
BARROW	1109	963		1190	939	870	2144	1047	1482	1194	1291	1081
BATH C	761	739	781		956	788	1156	693	762	983	649	993
BRAINTREE t	605	620	685	703		2029	864	697	1005	1005	650	1006
CAMBRIDGE	2482	2741	1651	2267	3717		2300	1911	2555	2408	2344	2436
DARLINGTON	1680	1965	1736	1420	2268	1784		1796	5638	1693	2581	2212
EBBSFLEET	875	687	983	816	938	964	1087		974	889	947	1143
FLEETWOOD	1686	1929	2091	1651	1791	2068	1811	1411		1687	1388	2447
FOREST GREEN	632	764	1070	1364	1033	1005	1131	1058	922		751	1181
GATESHEAD	606	991	701	512	745	904	1522	754	768	579		1132
GRIMSBY T	3704	2941	2675	3836	3688	2616	2887	2818	4061	3294	2938	
HAYES/Y	307	262	313	172	209	336	550	266	264	251	218	392
KETTERING	939	1093	896	1096	1115	2000	924	1402	1209	830	804	1354
KIDDMSTER	2440	1939	2135	1472	1301	1899	1635	1788	2341	2491	1636	1807
LINCOLN	2438	2253	2090	2244	1616	1978	2274	2111	2332	2076	1587	5506
LUTON T	5399	5658	5613	5745	5703	6274	5952	5526	6361	6061	6285	6419
MANSFIELD	2431	2982	2510	3997	1790	2046	1697	2630	3132	2008	1513	2982
NEWPORT	1540	1239	1315	1130	1101	1515	1249	1442	1011	1325	1261	1675
SOUTHPORT	1123	1061	1204	1021	938	1104	847	1231	2589	978	957	1934
STOCKPORT	2831	2802	3301	3744	3199	5957	2671	3674	3023	3391	2366	3943
TAMWORTH	1316	1241	1222	957	742	1137	977	921	958	783	968	892
WREXHAM	5812	4673	3432	3583	3303	4206	3171	2849	4283	4451	3161	2917
YORK CITY	2723	3166	3075	2030	2640	2711	2834	2973	4048	3391	2683	3872

BLUE SQUARE CONFERENCE   2011-12   ATTENDANCES (2)

HOME TEAMS / AWAY TEAMS	HAYES/YEADING	KETTERING	KIDDERMINSTER	LINCOLN C	LUTON TOWN	MANSFIELD T	NEWPORT CO	SOUTHPORT	STOCKPORT CO	TAMWORTH	WREXHAM	YORK CITY
AFC TELFORD	1941	2035	2192	2323	2640	2203	2147	2025	2375	3477	4591	1601
ALFRETON	600	851	990	1232	1654	3354	579	777	1115	1012	1165	1603
BARROW	1074	1090	1246	1181	925	1244	900	918	2103	1371	1463	2190
BATH CITY	512	734	676	760	1158	816	1147	663	919	656	1075	565
BRAINTREE	454	730	610	1182	1703	875	786	637	833	840	957	1127
CAMBRIDGE	1778	2578	2171	2875	4796	1738	1815	1840	2047	2281	3014	2211
DARLINGTON	1809	1742	1763	2252	1382	2647	1785	1637	2202	1752	1401	643
EBBSFLEET	1176	957	731	1217	1651	1085	992	907	1119	746	990	1522
FLEETWOOD	1376	1221	1316	4511	4446	3106	1277	3029	3021	1911	4994	2111
FOREST GREEN	781	823	1542	969	975	893	1203	873	1868	732	1109	1157
GATESHEAD	465	661	724	870	703	825	704	737	866	770	1258	1604
GRIMSBY T	2835	2470	3194	6672	3239	2553	2701	3738	2254	3206	3515	4250
HAYES IY		253	289	327	1015	487	303	294	654	359	625	525
KETTERING	1119		1301	1417	3247	1818	2047	1368	1281	1955	1377	1595
KIDDMSTER	1732	1967		2081	3332	3565	2275	1763	1886	1797	2492	2417
LINCOLN	2585	2269	2448		2049	2944	1951	1615	2152	2213	2211	3048
LUTON T	6003	7164	8445	6316		5261	6108	5681	5588	5833	7270	5925
MANSFIELD	1872	2051	2522	4830	2592		2324	2406	3883	2221	3665	3551
NEWPORT	1519	1249	1672	1270	1511	1285		1576	1205	1310	1431	1241
SOUTHPORT	1147	753	1544	1687	1665	1006	1105		1648	1310	1710	1107
STOCKPORT	2804	3424	3728	3975	3389	3571	3565	4540		6393	4518	3753
TAMWORTH	742	1197	924	1232	1467	1600	815	830	1381		1923	1012
WREXHAM	3845	4066	4102	3424	4206	3478	4232	3256	3874	3353		3872
YORK CITY	2603	2899	2830	3155	3570	4284	2824	3465	3370	2249	4295	

ABOUT THE AUTHOR

Paul (Scott) Wilson was born in the quiet village of Roecliffe, North Yorkshire, in 1956. He has lived there all his life. In 1983 he cycled across America from New York to Los Angeles to raise money for Charity. His first book, describing his epic journey, *The Sunshine Boys of Timoteo Canyon* was published in May 2009.

Paul has been an avid supporter of York City since 1967, and has been a season ticket holder at the club since 1974.